Forms of Address
for correspondence and conversation

Copyright © Templar Publishing Ltd 1988

First published in Great Britain in 1988
by Ward Lock Limited, 8 Clifford Street,
London W1X 1RB
An Egmont Company

Designed and produced by Templar Publishing Ltd
107 High Street, Dorking, Surrey RH4 1QA

Typeset by Servis Filmsetting Ltd, Manchester
Printed and bound in Great Britain
by Richard Clay Ltd, Chichester, Sussex

British Library Cataloguing in Publication Data
Webster, Jennifer
    Forms of address for correspondence and conversation.
    1. Forms of address & titles
    I. Title
    395′.4

ISBN 0–7063–6721–9

Forms of Address
for correspondence and conversation

Jennifer Webster

Ward Lock Limited · London

Contents

1. Introduction

There may be only one occasion in your life when you will need to know how to address an archbishop's wife or the younger son of a duke. If the moment occurs when you are standing on a public platform or about to write an important letter, such knowledge is a great comfort.

Knowing the correct form of address not only spares you embarrassment but also gives you confidence. During this century there has been a steady movement towards greater informality. This book reflects this trend, and the simpler forms of address are shown wherever possible. However, there are events which demand the strictest adherence to protocol, and these are described in full. Wherever relevant, both written and verbal styles are included, and the form of address is placed in a formal and a social context.

Forms of address in the United Kingdom are a unique blend of tradition and old-fashioned courtesy. There are many traps to catch the unwary. The information contained in this book is intended to steer you through this minefield and prepare you for any situation.

With a few exceptions (such as royalty), all the names, businesses and addresses are imaginary.

2. The business world

Business correspondence

First impressions

Business correspondence is written in a style which emphasises clarity and direct communication. Although this has great advantages, it does tend to make one letter look much like another. A certain anonymity is unavoidable, but it is wise to remember that, in many instances, your letter is the only impression an organisation has of you and therefore should be written with care.

It is most important, when writing to any firm or organisation, that your letter finds its way to the correct individual. When dealing with large organisations this is not always easy. If your letter is not correctly addressed or is lacking in clarity, it may travel around several departments before someone takes the responsibility for replying to you. Find out the name of the individual or department to whom your letter should be addressed. This may require a phone call or a visit to the library, but it will save time in the long run.

Business letters are built around a formal framework which gives cohesion to your correspondence. The style which you adopt in the content should reflect the tone of your letter. If the letter is one of enquiry, confirmation or thanks, a generally courteous tone would be in order. This can be done without straying into archaic terms which are no longer used in modern business practice. Phrases such as 'your esteemed interest' or 'acknowledge herewith the receipt of . . .' do nothing to improve a letter and may actually make it more tedious to read. It is possible to be friendly and courteous without resorting to old-fashioned terms. Similarly, letters of complaint or demand need not be overtly hostile. Brevity and a certain measured politeness may be much more effective.

The address

The address of the sender may appear in any position at the
top of the page: left, right or middle. If a printed letterhead is
used, it may also incorporate a telephone number, the VAT
number and the company registration. Many businesses also
include some sort of logo at the top of the page, as well as a
description of the nature of the company's business. The name
of the town usually appears in capitals, followed by the
postcode, which is never punctuated –

Root and Branch Ltd. (Tree Surgeons)
3 Oak Lane,
STAINES,
FS1 7TY
Tel: 0673 223

Reference

After the letterhead and the telephone number there may
appear a reference. This is to identify the letter for filing
purposes, and should be quoted in any reply.

Date

The date should not be abbreviated and should include the
day, month and year –

3rd. September 1988

Addressee

The name of the individual or the company to whom the letter
is addressed is placed immediately before the opening
salutation, together with the address. If the name is not
known, the job title of the addressee should be used, such as
'The Sales Director', or 'The Managing Director'. When
writing to a company, another line may follow the address
which indicates that the letter is 'For the Attention of . . .' a
particular person or department.

Opening the letter

If one firm is writing to another, or an individual to an organisation, the letter may begin 'Gentlemen'. This is, however, a rather old-fashioned greeting and would normally be replaced by 'Dear Sirs'.

When writing to an individual within a business, 'Dear Sir' or 'Dear Madam' would be used. For those who are known personally to the writer the greeting may be informal: 'Dear Mr Tillin' or 'Dear Mrs McKenzie'. First names would rarely be used, unless the letter was more personal than is usually the case in business correspondence. Even in the case of people known to the writer personally, they should be addressed by their job title or surname in formal correspondence. The plural of 'Madam' – 'Mesdames' – is not used, and should be replaced wherever possible by the name of an individual or by 'Dear Madam'.

Subject heading

When writing about a specific matter or with regard to an account, the subject is typed under the opening of the letter, to the left or in the centre, and underlined.

Dear Sir,

Our Order No.3998

Ending the letter

The manner in which a letter is closed is dictated by the greeting. If the letter has begun 'Dear Sir', 'Dear Madam' or 'Dear Sirs', it should end 'Yours faithfully'. When the letter is opened by name, the ending is 'Yours sincerely'.

The signature

Letters should always be signed by hand. It is usual in business circles to follow this with a typed version of the name. This prevents confusion and allows the addition of the person's position within the company.

Yours faithfully,

Martin Jessop

Martin Jessop
Chief Accountant

There may be occasions when a person has to sign a letter on behalf of another. Where there are a great many letters to sign in this way the letters 'pp' are placed before the name of the writer and the letter is signed by another –

Yours faithfully,

Helen Jay.

pp Martin Jessop

Two other alternatives would be –

Yours faithfully,

Helen Jay.

For Martin Jessop
or –
Yours faithfully,

Helen Jay.

Dictated by Martin Jessop and signed in his absence

Where a letter has been written on behalf of another person, this is also made clear. A secretary who has been instructed by her senior to write a letter will sign it herself –

Yours faithfully,

Helen Jay.

Helen Jay (Mrs)
Secretary to
Martin Jessop

Certain letters should not be signed by junior staff. These include replies to serious complaints, letters of sympathy or those of a personal nature. It is preferable that letters of condolence be written by hand.

Enclosures

If there are any enclosures, this is indicated beneath the signature, together with the number if more than one –

```
      Enc
or – Encs 3
```

Additional pages

The number of the page should be typed at the top, either to the left or in the centre. The date and the addressee should be repeated.

Carbon copies

If copies of a letter are to be sent to others, this is noted at the end of the letter –

c.c. H.V. Yates

or –

Copies to: C.M. Unwin
D.B. Sherrif
A.S. Lowe

There may be occasions when copies are sent without the knowledge of the addressee. If this is the case, the notation is omitted from the top copy.

The right address

Delayed mail can cause frustration and reflects badly on the efficiency of a firm. Prompt delivery of mail is made much easier if a letter or parcel is correctly addressed and carries the required postage. Marking a letter 'URGENT' and then sending it by 'second class' mail will not create the best of impressions.

If the letter is to go directly to an individual, this must be clearly indicated by the words 'Private and Confidential' typed above the name on the envelope.

The address should be written on the lower half of the envelope and typed. The correct order is –

The name of the addressee	Mr K.H. Gordon
or the business position	The Marketing Manager
The name of the firm	Gordon Enterprises
The number/name and the street, etc.	71, Woodley Avenue
Locality or village	Meadowhurst
Postal town (in capitals)	GRANGETOWN
Postcode	XV6 9MG

The postcode should always be typed in capitals, without punctuation, and with a space separating the two parts.

Finding the right person

Writing to the 'unknown' can be a problem. The structure of companies varies, and it may be difficult finding out who should deal with your enquiry.

The board of directors
Limited companies are usually run by a board of directors who decide on policy matters. Their meetings are presided over by a chairman of the board, who may be a part-time, but highly experienced, member of the company.

The managing director
The actual implementation of the company's policies is undertaken by the managing director. It is a good idea to address your letter to him or her if the subject relates to the company as a whole.

Managers and heads of departments
Particular areas of responsibility are given to departmental managers, and it may be that your letter should be addressed to them if it falls within such categories as sales, marketing, publicity, planning, accounts and finance.

The personnel officer
In most companies this post covers a wide area of responsibility. The personnel officer should be contacted if the query relates to recruitment, training, holidays, health and safety, or the general welfare of the staff.

The company secretary
Limited companies are required to have a company secretary, whose task it is to monitor the company's activities and to see that it fulfils its legal requirements.

Messrs

The term 'Messrs' is not in general use, although it may still be used in correspondence with the legal profession. It is only used where personal names constitute the name of the firm. The names should either be all male or men and women together, for example –

> Messrs   Kenneth & Jeremy Ironside
> Messrs   Frederick Kimberley & Sons
> Messrs   Talbot, Rickards & Porter

If the surname is only part of the company's name, or if it is a limited company, the term should not be used. In firms where all the partners are women, 'Messrs' is not used. The envelope would read –

> Gainsborough & Daughters
> Henrietta & Denise Wright

Business partnerships

When a business is run jointly by several partners, it is usual to place the name of the senior partner first. In the firm of Messrs Mason, Makepeace & Windthrop Mr Mason is the senior partner.

If another partner is taken into a firm, it does not necessarily mean that the name of the firm will change, especially if there are already several existing partners. An announcement may be made to the following effect –

> Messrs Mason, Makepeace and Windthrop have pleasure in announcing that, as from 1st. January 1988, they will be taking into partnership Mr Alistair MacKinley, C.A. The name of the firm will remain unchanged.

Letters of introduction

Occasionally business contacts are introduced by a letter of introduction. They are usually placed in an unsealed envelope, unless the letter has to be posted. An example –

> Dear Mr Goode,
>
> The bearer of this letter, Mr Jeremy Haig, is the senior partner in the firm of Messrs Haig, Leigh & Company, who are good business friends of mine and of high standing in this region.
>
> Mr Haig is visiting your district during the coming month to establish business contacts, and I shall be grateful if you will assist him in any way you can.
>
> Yours sincerely,

References and testimonials

Most applications for jobs or for membership of a club or society are accompanied by the names of referees. Such names should never be given without first asking the permission of the person concerned. As a referee is usually required to give some assessment of character as well as ability, it is important to choose a referee from people who know you well.

Open testimonials are usually placed in an unsealed envelope and addressed 'To whom it may concern'. They are often written when a candidate requires a reference for use in the future or for a purpose as yet unspecified.

A confidential reference tends to carry more weight than a testimonial, as it is written with the utmost frankness. Such references should always be addressed to a specific individual and marked 'Private and Confidential'. When this is not possible, the recipient should be indicated by office, for example, the personnel officer or a head of department.

It is not unusual for a written reference to be followed up by a telephone call from a prospective employer. This may occur, however, if the reference has been a little ambiguous or if there is any indecision over the selection of a candidate. Such calls should be taken in private, as they are as much in confidentiality as the original letter.

Business cards

A business card has quite specific functions: it details the professional qualifications of the bearer and the nature of his employment. He or she may be the representative of a company or be self-employed. Either a business or home address, or both, should be included, together with a telephone number. The examples shown contain the basic information necessary, although the design may vary.

Gabrielle Dupont
Worldwide Travel Service

75, The Avenue
Hammersmith,
W6   01 660 4499

Captain Neil Mainwaring
Royal Navy (Retd.)

Plainsail Yachts Ltd.
Plymouth
Devon
Tel: 0243 856

TERENCE DERBY F.R.P.S.
Professional Photographer

Paradise Studios
Haverford Way
Norwich
56 789564

4, Rose Mews
Manor Close
Fordbridge
Norfolk
098 456 3546

Internal memos and invitations

The internal memorandum

An internal memorandum, or 'memo', may be used for
communication within a firm for a variety of reasons. It may
contain a message from one manager or executive to another,
or from the management to the work force. It is less formal
than a letter and does not include the address, greeting or
signature.

INTERNAL MEMORANDUM

TO All members of Staff   *DATE* 8 June 88

FROM Personnel Manager   *REF* PM/ST

I am sure that you will all be greatly relieved to know that our office heating equipment has at last been repaired. The last few weeks have not been easy ones, and I know that many of you have suffered from the fluctuations in the temperature of the offices. Thanks for your cooperation and the uncomplaining manner in which you have conducted the day-to-day business.

BCH
Pers Man

INTERNAL MEMORANDUM

TO Derek Wall   *DATE* 17 July 88

FROM Clive Allenby   *REF* CA/17

YUMMYCHEWS PROMOTION
I have confirmed with the M.D. that this promotion can be launched together with the Mintygum promotion at the end of August. I hope that this will give you enough time to complete the organisation of the sales team. I will pass on any further information as I have it.

CA
Publ. Dept.

Business invitations

Invitations may be sent to individuals or groups within a business. Important occasions such as the annual dinner are usually printed on card, but less formal occasions may be covered by a friendly letter of invitation. Both formal and informal invitations should state the date, time and place of the event, as well as detailing the nature of the occasion, as in the following example –

The Managing Director
of the Crunchy Biscuit Company Limited
requests the pleasure of the company of
Mr and Mrs Stephen White
at the Centenary Dinner
at the Russell Hotel, Fell Road, Southsea
on Friday 8th September 1988 at 8.00p.m.

The Managing Director
Crunchy Biscuit Company Ltd.
Valley Trading Estate
Southsea   R.S.V.P.

An acceptance to attend this event may be worded –

Mr and Mrs Stephen White
thank the Managing Director
of the Crunchy Biscuit Company Limited
for his invitation to the centenary dinner
at the Russell Hotel on Friday 8th September
and have much pleasure in accepting.

Less formal invitations may be extended by letter –

THE CRUNCHY BISCUIT COMPANY LIMITED
Valley Trading Estate, Southsea

Directors: Telephone 0785 776598
K.M. Smiley
V.N. Hume
R.P. Lang

IN/67   12th August 1988

The Sales Director
Decor Tins Ltd.
54, Madeley Street
Southsea

Dear Mr Williams

Our company celebrates one hundred years of
trading this year and we plan to mark this occasion
by holding a centenary dinner.

Over the years our company has enjoyed a close and
amicable business relationship with Decor Tins, and
we would like to take this opportunity to invite you
and your sales team to this event. It will be held at the
Russell Hotel on Friday 8th September at 8.00p.m.

It would be helpful if you could give us your reply as
soon as possible so that arrangements may be
finalised.

Yours sincerely

Richard Lang
Marketing Director

Using the telephone

Using the correct form of address is as important in speech as in writing. The telephone is often the first line of approach to a business and getting through to the right person is not always easy. A pencil and paper should always be available to write down a name. Don't hesitate to ask for a name to be repeated or spelt if it is hard to understand. Even the most straightforward name can have variations (Brown or Browne). Whoever answers the telephone should say the name of the company. If you do not know the name of the person with whom you wish to speak, ask for him or her by title or department: 'I would like to speak to the person in charge of your publicity department, please.'

If that person is not available, you could ask to speak to someone else in the same department. Alternatively, you could ring back later. If you decide to do this, make sure that you have the name or extension number before you ring off. Once you have located the correct person or department, give your name before beginning to explain the nature of your call. If the person or department cannot take your call at that moment, you may wish to leave a message. If so, make sure that you give all the relevant information to the person passing it on –

Miss Georgina Burns in the Finance Department was called by Mr Roland Jennings of H.M. Customs and Excise – Tel. 348 7639. He wishes to make an appointment to inspect the VAT figures and would appreciate a return call by Thursday a.m.

Call taken by Matthew Worth at 11.00a.m.

3. The academic world

The universities

The hierarchy of administration may vary slightly in the 46 universities of the United Kingdom. These are self-governing bodies and are usually headed by a chancellor. The executive head of a university may be the vice-chancellor or the principal, the rector or the president. In the academic world they are referred to by office.

Chancellors of universities

Outside the university a chancellor is known by his name or rank, but for the purpose of his office he would be addressed as follows –

Written
ENVELOPE
Formal   The Chancellor of the University of Leeds
Social   Sir Luke Downing, K.B.E., M.A.
               Chancellor of the University of Leeds

LETTER
Formal   *Begin*   Sir or Dear Chancellor or My Lord (if a peer)
             End   Yours faithfully
Social   *Begin*   Dear Sir Luke or Dear Chancellor
             End   Yours sincerely

Spoken
Formal   Mr Chancellor (at official functions) or Sir Luke
Social   Sir Luke or Chancellor
The description in conversation is 'The Chancellor'.

Vice-chancellors

In the main, vice-chancellors are addressed in the same fashion as a chancellor. The exceptions to this are the vice-chancellors of Oxford and Cambridge who are styled –

The Revd. the Vice-Chancellor of the University of Oxford
The Right Worshipful the Vice-Chancellor of the University of Cambridge.
These forms of address would only be used in the context of university matters.

High stewards

This office is held within the universities of Oxford and Cambridge. The holder is addressed by his name or rank on matters outside the university –
The Lord Bradenshaw P.C., C.M.G., O.B.E., M.A.
For the purposes of university business, the correct style is –

Written

ENVELOPE	The High Steward of the University of Oxford	
LETTER		
Formal	*Begin*	Dear High Steward or Sir
	End	Yours faithfully
Social	*Begin*	Dear High Steward
	End	Yours sincerely
Spoken	According to rank	

Heads of colleges

Like the heads of universities, heads of colleges are also known by a variety of titles, according to the tradition of the university. They may be styled the Dean, Director, Master, Mistress, President, Principal, Provost, Warden or Rector. During their term of office they are addressed by title or name.

Written

ENVELOPE   The Mistress (or relevant title)
Girton College,
Cambridge
or, less formally –
Lady Jane Dedhan Ph.D
Mistress of Girton College,
Cambridge

LETTER

Formal	*Begin*	Madam or Sir
	End	Yours faithfully
Social	*Begin*	Dear Director, Warden, etc.
	End	Yours sincerely
Spoken		At Oxford and Cambridge the style is 'Mr Dean' or 'Mr Warden', otherwise 'Sir', 'Madam' or by name or office.

Clergymen are addressed by their ecclesiastical title before their academic office.

Professors

Written

ENVELOPE	Professor Gilbert Bembridge
'Professor'	precedes any other title held, such as –
	Professor Lord Tenby
	or Professor the Hon. Derek Hewett

LETTER

Formal	*Begin*	Dear Sir or Madam
	End	Yours faithfully
Social	*Begin*	Dear Professor Bembridge

However, if the professor is a peer or holds a knighthood, he is addressed by rank, for example – Dear Sir Gilbert.

	End	
		Yours sincerely
Spoken		Professor Bembridge (unless he holds a title)

After retirement a Professor may be styled 'Professor Emeritus'. In correspondence the forms of address are as before.

Other university ranks

Other university offices include those of registrar, proctor and bursar. If the correspondence relates to university business, they may be addressed by title or name.

Degrees

All universities are empowered to award degrees. The name of the degree, in abbreviated form, is placed after the holder's name. There is some variance in the relative importance placed on these qualifications. Some universities place their degrees in ascending order, with first degrees (generally 'bachelor') preceding higher degrees (generally 'master' then 'doctor'). Others put them in descending order. If in doubt it is best to check with the awarding body. Abbreviations for degrees are listed in Appendix 2.

Doctors

Holders of doctorates are styled 'Doctor'. Whether they wish to adopt this style or to have the appropriate letters for their particular doctorate placed after their name is a matter of preference. Doctors of Divinity would normally opt for the latter and use their ecclesiastical style before their name. Letters indicating a doctorate are often used as a suffix to the name to make it clear that the holder is not a doctor of medicine.

Written

ENVELOPE	Keith Young Esq. Ph.D
	The Very Rev. Lionel Downing D.D
	Lord Kinclair LL.D
LETTER	
Formal	*Begin* Dear Sir or Madam
	End Yours faithfully
Social	*Begin* Dear Doctor Young
	or by title, Dear Lord Kinclair
	End Yours sincerely
Spoken	Dr Young or Lord Kinclair

Honorary doctorates

Holders of honorary doctorates may be styled 'Doctor', if this is their wish. It should not be used to imply that this is an academic qualification.

Doctors of Medicine

Those styled 'Doctor' in the medical profession are not always the holder of a doctorate. They are, however, addressed as such by courtesy and tradition, even though the final degree has not been taken. In written forms of address their qualifications would be shown after their name.

Titled doctors are addressed by rank.

Written

ENVELOPE   Dr Michael Pearson
            or Michael Pearson Esq., M.D., F.R.C.P.
            or Michael Pearson, Esq., B.M., B.A.

LETTER

Formal   *Begin*   Dear Sir
           End   Yours faithfully

Social   *Begin*   Dear Doctor Pearson
           End   Yours sincerely

Spoken   Dr Pearson

Surgeons

A surgeon is addressed both in correspondence and speech as 'Mr'. The address on the envelope would be –

           Robert Joyce, Esq. M.S., F.C.P.S.

In England and Wales, obstetricians and gynaecologists are addressed in the same manner as surgeons.

Pathologists, radiologists and anaesthetists are addressed as 'Doctor'.

Fellowships

Honorary fellowships would usually be indicated in correspondence. If, however, the fellowship is by subscription it is only included if the correspondence concerns that particular field of interest.

Other educational institutions

Heads of schools and colleges

Heads of schools, colleges and other educational
establishments are referred to by their office if the
correspondence concerns an educational matter –

The Headmistress,
The Warden
The Principal

It is also acceptable to address the head by name.
Appointments are usually styled as follows –

Girls' schools
Headmistress or Principal

Boys' schools
Headmaster or High Master

Technical and tertiary colleges
Principal or Warden

Teaching hospitals, medical schools and colleges
Dean or Principal

Adult education centres
Warden

Central institutions in Scotland
Principal or Director

Polytechnics
Principal or Director

There may, of course be variations. If in doubt, a telephone
call to the secretary of the establishment will clarify the
situation.

4. The law

The judiciary in England and Wales

The supreme legal authority in England and Wales is the House of Lords. The Lord Chancellor and the Law Lords (Lords of Appeal in Ordinary) form the ultimate Court of Appeal.

Lord Chancellor

On appointment, the Lord Chancellor is raised to the peerage. His responsibilities are many: he is Speaker of the House of Lords, President of the Court of Appeal, a Privy Counsellor and the chief judicial officer in England and Wales.

Written

ENVELOPE	The Rt. Hon. the Lord Chancellor	
LETTER		
Formal	*Begin*	My Lord
	End	Yours faithfully
Social	*Begin*	Dear Lord Chancellor
	End	Yours sincerely
Spoken	Lord Chancellor or by rank	

Lord Chief Justice

The recipient of this title is raised to the peerage and becomes a Privy Counsellor. He is President of the Criminal Division of the Court of Appeal, which hears appeals from the Crown Courts, and is head of the Queen's Bench Division.

Written

ENVELOPE	The Rt. Hon. the Lord Chief Justice of England	
LETTER		
Formal	*Begin*	My Lord
	End	Yours faithfully
Social	*Begin*	Dear Lord Chief Justice

	End	Yours sincerely
Spoken		According to his rank

Master of the Rolls

The Master of the Rolls receives a knighthood on appointment and is a member of the Privy Council. He is President of the Civil Division of the Court of Appeal which hears appeals from the High Courts and County Courts. He is addressed by his rank in the judiciary.

Lord Justices of the Court of Appeal

These are appointed to sit with the Master of the Rolls and are usually knights. Q.C. is not written after their name.

Written

ENVELOPE   The Rt. Hon. Lord Justice Jones
LETTER
Formal   *Begin*   My Lord
            End   Yours faithfully
Social   *Begin*   Dear Lord Justice
            End   Yours sincerely

Spoken

Formal   My Lord or Your Lordship
Social   Lord Justice

Formally and socially he may be described in conversation as The Lord Justice or Lord Justice Jones. In court he is styled 'His Lordship'.

If two Lord Justices share the same surname, the form of address for the junior of the two will include his forename to avoid confusion, such as –

Lord Justice Jones
Lord Justice Sebastian Jones

Lords of Appeal

When the House of Lords is acting in its judicial capacity, the Lords of Appeal in Ordinary preside. They are Privy Counsellors and life peers. They are addressed in the style of a baron (see Chapter 10), and never have the letters Q.C. following their name.

High Court judges

It is usual for a judge of the High Court to receive a knighthood on appointment. Women High Court judges are created Dames. The abbreviation Q.C. does not follow their name.

Written

ENVELOPE

Formal and on judicial matters
> The Hon. Mr Justice Walker
> The Hon. Mrs Justice Grenville (also used by an unmarried judge)

Social
> Sir Bernard Walker
> Dame Diana Grenville

LETTER

Formal	*Begin*	Sir or Dear Sir
		Madam or Dear Madam
	End	Yours faithfully
Social	*Begin*	Dear Judge
		Dear Dame Diana
	End	Yours sincerely
Judicially	*Begin*	My Lord or My Lady

Spoken

Formal	Sir
	Madam
In court	My Lord or Your Lordship
	My Lady or Your Ladyship
Social	Sir Bernard
	Dame Diana
	or Judge (often used by barristers)

Retired High Court judges

Written

ENVELOPE   Sir Robin Harris or Dame Alice Webb

LETTER

Formal	*Begin*	Sir or Dear Sir
		Madam or Dear Madam
	End	Yours faithfully
Social	*Begin*	Dear Judge or Dear Sir Robin
		or Dear Dame Alice
	End	Yours sincerely

Spoken

| Formal | Sir or Madam |
| Social | Judge or Sir Robin or Dame Alice |

Circuit judges

Written

ENVELOPE   His (or Her) Honour Judge Hammill
If the judge has a knighthood he is addressed as –
                 His Honour Judge Sir Jeffrey Hammill
or socially as Sir Jeffrey Hammill. If the judge has been a
Queen's Counsel, Q.C. follows the name.

LETTER

Formal	*Begin*	Sir or Dear Sir
		Madam or Dear Madam
	End	Yours faithfully
Social	*Begin*	Dear Judge
	End	Yours sincerely

Spoken

Formal	Sir or Madam
In court	Your Honour
Social	Judge or Sir Jeffrey

On retirement a circuit judge may still be styled 'His or
Her Honour'. The title of 'Judge' is no longer used.

Justices of the Peace

A Justice of the Peace is addressed by his or her name or
rank, unless in court, when the style is 'Your Worship'. The
letters J.P. may follow the name when writing to a justice in
his or her official capacity. A solicitor or barrister who is a
stipendiary magistrate does not have J.P. after his name.

Coroners

A coroner is addressed by name, except when in court, when he is styled 'Sir'.

Recorders

Written
ENVELOPE
When the letter relates to official matters –
            Peter Kavanagh, Esq., Q.C.,
            Recorder of Pemberton
Otherwise– Peter Kavanagh, Esq., Q.C.
LETTER

Formal	*Begin*	Sir or Dear Sir
		or Dear Mr Recorder
	End	Yours faithfully
Social	*Begin*	Dear Mr Kavanagh
	End	Yours sincerely

Spoken
In court   Sir

Mr Kavanagh or by rank.

The Attorney General

As head of the Bar in England, the Attorney General takes precedence over barristers. Both he and the Solicitor General have the letters Q.C. following their name.

Barristers and Queen's Counsel

A barrister is not afforded any special title unless he becomes a Queen's Counsel (also known as 'taking silk'). The abbreviation Q.C. follows the name of a Queen's Counsel for the period that he or she is at the bar. Judges, apart from circuit judges, do not add Q.C. to their names.

The police force

Metropolitan Police Commissioner

Written
ENVELOPE   Sir Stuart Canning

or Stephen Dearn, Esq.
Commissioner of Police of the Metropolis

LETTER

Formal   *Begin*   Sir or Dear Sir
            End   Yours faithfully

Social   *Begin*   Dear Sir Stuart
                     or Dear Mr Dearn
                     or Dear Commissioner
            End   Yours sincerely

Spoken   Commissioner or Mr Dearn

A deputy commissioner would have his particular title on the envelope. In both cases the relevant decorations are placed after the name.

Commander, chief superintendent, superintendent

Officers of these ranks are addressed by name or rank. On envelopes the rank may precede the name or follow it –

           Chief Superintendent M.G. Scott, M.B.E.,
           City of London Police
or   Mark V. Scott, Esq., M.B.E.,
           Chief Superintendent, City of London Police

A woman superintendent would be addressed on the envelope as follows –

           W/Chief Superintendent K.L. Hatton

C.I.D. officers' titles are preceded by 'Detective'.

Chief inspectors, inspectors

The rank, both for men and women, is placed before the name on the envelope.

Police sergeant and police constable

These ranks are often abbreviated –

           P.S. or W.P.S. Hawkins
           P.C. or W.P.C. Hawkins

Chief Constables

Written

ENVELOPE   Sir Andrew Cooper

LETTER
Formal   *Begin*   Sir or Dear Sir
            End   Yours faithfully
Social   *Begin*   Dear Chief Constable
                     or Dear Sir Andrew
            End   Yours sincerely
Spoken   Chief Constable or Sir Andrew

The judiciary in Scotland

Scotland operates a separate judiciary system from that of
England and Wales. The system of public prosecution is
headed by the Lord Advocate and is independent of the police
force.

Lord Justice-General

Written
ENVELOPE   The Rt. Hon. the Lord Justice-General
LETTER
Formal   *Begin*   My Lord
            End   Yours faithfully
Social   *Begin*   Dear Lord Justice-General
            End   Yours sincerely

Spoken
Formal   My Lord
Social   Lord Justice-General
     The wife of the Lord Justice-General is addressed as the
wife of a baron (see Chapter 10).

Lord Justice-Clerk

If a Privy Counsellor, the holder of this appointment is
styled –
                 The Rt. Hon. the Lord Justice-Clerk
Otherwise, as – The Hon. the Lord Justice-Clerk
His wife is addressed as the wife of a baron (see Chapter 10).

Lord of Session

A Lord of Session is a judge or senator of the Scottish College of Justice.

Written

ENVELOPE   The Hon. Lord Robinson
                or The Rt. Hon., if a Privy Counsellor

LETTER

Formal	*Begin*	My Lord
	End	Your faithfully
Social	*Begin*	Dear Lord Robinson
	End	Yours sincerely

Spoken

| Formal | My Lord |
| Social | Lord Robinson |

   Lords of Session are addressed after their retirement in the same manner.

Lord Advocate

The Lord Advocate may be a member of either of the two Houses of Parliament.

Written

ENVELOPE   The Rt. Hon. the Lord Advocate, Q.C., M.P.
                or The Rt. Hon. Gordon Burns, Q.C., M.P.

LETTER

Formal	*Begin*	My Lord (if a peer)
		or Dear Sir
	End	Yours faithfully
Social	*Begin*	Dear Lord Advocate (if a legal matter)
		or by name
	End	Yours sincerely

Spoken   My Lord (if a peer) or by name

Sheriffs Principal

Scotland is divided into six sheriffdoms, with resident sheriffs who are judges of the Sheriff Court. They are addressed as 'Sheriff ————', or in court as 'My Lord' or 'My Lady'.

5. The diplomatic service

Diplomatic missions provide a valuable means of communication between countries. The importance of the role of an ambassador or high commissioner is reflected by his or her position in the order of precedence. The forms of address used in diplomatic circles are amongst the most formal and elaborate in use today.

Foreign diplomats in the United Kingdom

Ambassadors

A foreign ambassador accredited to the United Kingdom is styled His/Her Excellency. This title precedes any service rank or title except that of His or Her Highness/Royal Highness/Serene Highness. The name of the country may be used in its adjectival form, but it may be preferable to use the full name, expecially when the adjectival form sounds clumsy.

Written

ENVELOPE   His Excellency
           The Ambassador of Italy
   or His Excellency
           The Italian Ambassador

When writing to an address other than the embassy, or if the letter is a private one, it is acceptable to write –
           His Excellency Signor Peroni

This may be followed by any initials, but never by 'Esquire'.

LETTER

Formal	*Begin*	Your Excellency
	End	I have the honour to be, with the highest consideration, Your Excellency's obedient servant
Social	*Begin*	Dear Ambassador
	End	Believe me, My dear Ambassador, Yours sincerely

Spoken

Formal	It is correct to use the term 'Your Excellency' at least once during a conversation. 'Sir' or the name is used thereafter.
Social	Ambassador, or by name – 'Signor Peroni'

When mentioning the ambassador in conversation, he is described, formally, as 'His Excellency'. Otherwise, 'The Ambassador', 'The German Ambassador' or, more simply, his name may be used.

The wife of an ambassador is not addressed as 'Your Excellency' except as a courtesy title. 'Ambassadress' may be used, but this must never be confused with the correct style for a lady ambassador.

High commissioners

A Commonwealth high commissioner is addressed within the United Kingdom as 'Your Excellency' and shares precedence with foreign ambassadors. A British high commissioner in a Commonwealth country is styled 'Excellency'.

Written

ENVELOPE	His Excellency	
	The High Commissioner for Australia	
LETTER		
Formal	*Begin*	Your Excellency
	End	I have the honour to be
		Your Excellency's obedient servant
Social	*Begin*	Dear High Commissioner
	End	Believe me,
		Yours sincerely

Spoken

Formal	'Your Excellency' at least once, and then by name or 'Sir'.
Social	'High Commissioner', or by name

British diplomats overseas

British ambassadors to foreign countries

Although such an ambassador may be styled 'Your Excellency' in other countries, he or she is not so styled in the United Kingdom. If the office is held by a woman she is addressed as 'Ambassador'. The husband or wife of the ambassador is not accorded any particular style, although a woman may be called 'Ambassadress' as a courtesy.

Written

ENVELOPE His Excellency Sir Toby Rowlands,
H.M. Ambassador,
British Embassy

LETTER

Formal	*Begin*	Sir, or Madam
	End	I have the honour to be, Sir/Madam, Your Excellency's obedient servant
Social	*Begin*	Dear Ambassador
	End	Believe me, My dear Ambassador, Yours sincerely

Spoken

Formal Initially 'Your Excellency', then 'Sir' or 'Madam'.
Social 'The Ambassador', or by name

Chargé d'affaires

A chargé d'affaires may take charge when the head of a diplomatic mission is absent. In Commonwealth countries such a position is undertaken by an acting high commissioner.

Written

ENVELOPE Norman Davidson, Esq.,
Chargé d'Affaires,
British Embassy

Lionel Richards, Esq.,
Acting High Commissioner,
British High Commission

Formal	*Begin*	Sir
	End	I have the honour to be,
		Sir,
		Your obedient servant
		or, if foreign –
		I have the honour to be,
		Sir,
		with high consideration,
		Your obedient servant
Social	*Begin*	Dear Chargé d'Affaires, or by name
	End	Yours sincerely
Spoken		Chargé d'Affaires, or by name

Consuls-general, consuls and vice-consuls

As a holder of Her Majesty's commission, any of these
officials may have the letters 'H.M.' before his or her name. If
the appointment is governmental, the title is 'The British
Consul'.

The form of address is as for 'Esquire' (see Chapter 12),
with the exception of the envelope, which would read –

Frederick Maddox,
H.M. Consul-General,
British Consulate-General

Governor-generals and governors

Within a territory administered by the United Kingdom, a
governor-general is styled 'His Excellency'. Governors and
lieutenant-governors of Jersey, Guernsey and the Isle of Man
share the same form of address. Only the wife of a governor-
general is styled 'Her Excellency' within her husband's
administered country.

Written

ENVELOPE   His Excellency
             Mr Alistair Gibson,
             Governor of Queensland

Other titles and ranks do not precede this form of address, for example –

             His Excellency
             Sir Ian Newbury, K.C.B.,
             Governor of Auckland

LETTER

Formal	*Begin*	Sir, or if a peer, My Lord
	End	I have the honour to be,
		Sir,
		Your Excellency's obedient servant
Social	*Begin*	Dear Mr Gibson
		Dear Sir Ian
	End	Yours sincerely

Spoken

Formal	Your Excellency
Social	By name

The British representative at the Holy See is called a minister although he is addressed as an ambassador. Other ministers may serve an ambassador within the larger embassies. They do not have any special form of address.

6. Government

Central government

Privy Counsellors

All members of the British Cabinet are Privy Counsellors, although the Privy Council may also include other ministers. A full council is summoned only on the death of the sovereign, or when the sovereign plans to marry. The Cabinet acts as a select committee of the Privy Council and is composed of heads of government departments, secretaries of state and other important offices.

When writing to a Privy Counsellor he or she is addressed as 'The Right Hon'. Husbands and wives of Privy Counsellors do not share the title.

Written

ENVELOPE   The Right Hon. William Walker
If the Privy Counsellor is an officer in the armed forces or has a position within the church, the envelope would read –

> Air Marshal The Right Hon. William Walker
> The Right Revd. and Right Hon. Lord Bishop of Exeter

If the Privy Counsellor is a woman, Mrs or Miss is omitted –

> The Right Hon. Charlotte Hayman

LETTER

Formal	*Begin*	Sir or Dear Sir or Dear Madam
	End	Yours faithfully
Social	*Begin*	Dear Mr Walker
	End	Yours faithfully
Spoken		Mr Walker
		or, if a woman –
		Mrs Charlotte Hayman

The Prime Minister

The Prime Minister is addressed as a Privy Counsellor.

Written

ENVELOPE   The Right Hon. Phillip Collins, M.P.

LETTER

Formal   *Begin*   Dear Sir or Dear Madam

            End   Yours faithfully

Social   *Begin*   Dear Prime Minister

            End   Yours sincerely

Spoken   Prime Minister, or by name

Ministers of H.M. government

Written

ENVELOPE   Personal letters to his or her department are
addressed –
The Rt. Hon. Toby Westwood, M.P.,
Secretary of State for Education

If the letter is to a minister with regard to his departmental
status, the address includes his or her appointment only –
Secretary of State for the Environment

The Speaker of the House of Commons

He is addressed according to his rank unless it concerns a
parliamentary matter, in which case he is styled 'Mr Speaker'.
As a general rule, however, it is not modern practice to place
'Mr' or 'Mrs' before an offical title.

Members of Parliament

M.P.s are addressed as ordinary persons with the addition of
'M.P.' following the name. Privy Counsellors are addressed as
'The Right Hon.', unless they are afforded this title in their
own right. In this case, P.C. is placed after the name.

The civil service

The form of address may vary according to the matter in
question. If your letter concerns an important matter, it
should be addressed to the ministerial head of the department.
Minor matters are sent to 'The Secretary' of the department.

Written

Formal	*Begin*	(within the civil service) Sir or Madam
		Dear Sir or Dear Madam
	End	I have the honour to be,
		Sir,
		Yours faithfully
		or Yours faithfully
Social	*Begin*	Dear Under-Secretary
		or Dear Mr Hewett
	End	Your sincerely
Spoken		By name or appointment

Local government in England and Wales

Outside Greater London, England is divided into counties and, within these, districts. There are also six large metropolitan counties, which are further divided into 36 metropolitan districts. Greater London is composed of 32 London boroughs plus the City of London. Councils are elected to these divisions and each division elects a chairman.

When writing to the local council on matters of major policy, letters should be addressed to the chairman or the council as a whole. Particular aspects of local government, such as education or recreation, may be addressed to the chairman of the relevant committee. Alternatively, residents may contact the councillor for the ward in which they live.

Lord-lieutenants and lieutenants of counties

Both these appointments are representatives of the queen for the county to which they are designated. They are addressed by their normal title, except in formal correspondence, when the envelope should read –

> Henry Boswell, Esq.,
> H.M. Lieutenant of Humberside

| ***Spoken*** | My Lord Lieutenant or Her Majesty's Lieutenant |

High sheriffs and sheriffs

A sheriff appointed by the queen is styled a 'High Sheriff' and takes responsibility for a particular county. His title is included in written correspondence –

> James Davenport, Esq.,
> High Sheriff of Suffolk

Sheriffs are elected by cities and perform mainly ceremonial duties. They have no special forms of address, although the appointment follows the name in official letters. The City of London has two sheriffs, who are normally aldermen. Official correspondence should be addressed as follows –

Written
ENVELOPE   Mr Alderman and Sheriff Thomas Black
LETTER   *Begin*   Dear Alderman and Sheriff
             End   Yours faithfully

Chairmen of county councils

Written
ENVELOPE   The Chairman of the Dorset County Council
              or by name if a personal letter
LETTER
Formal   *Begin*   Dear Mr Chairman (men and women)
             End   Yours faithfully
Social   *Begin*   Dear Mr Chairman
             End   Yours sincerely

Spoken
Formal   Mr Chairman (men and women)
Social   Mrs Edwards

Chairmen of district councils

These are addressed in a similar way to chairmen of county councils. Whether or not they are the civic head of the district varies according to the status of the district. Those with borough status elect mayors as the civic head.

Lord mayors

Forms of address are the same whether the title is held by a man or a woman. The lord mayors of London, York, Belfast and Cardiff are styled 'The Right Honourable'. Others are addressed as 'The Right Worshipful'.

Written

ENVELOPE   The Right Honourable the Lord Mayor of London
       or The Right Worshipful the Lord Mayor of Plymouth

LETTER

Formal   *Begin*   My Lord Mayor
        End   Yours faithfully
Social   *Begin*   Dear Lord Mayor
        End   Yours sincerely

Spoken

Formal   My Lord Mayor
Social   Lord Mayor

If the lord mayor is a married woman, her husband is known as 'The Lord Mayor's Consort'.

Lady mayoresses

A lady mayoress may be the wife, daughter or chosen female friend of the lord mayor. She does not share the style 'The Right Hon.' or 'The Right Worshipful'.

Written

ENVELOPE   The Lady Mayoress of York

LETTER

Formal   *Begin*   My Lady Mayoress
        End   Yours faithfully
Social   *Begin*   Dear Lady Mayoress
        End   Yours sincerely

Spoken

Formal   My Lady Mayoress
Social   Lady Mayoress

Mayors

The mayors of cities and some Cinque ports are styled 'The Right Worshipful'. Other mayors use the style 'The Worshipful'.

Written

ENVELOPE		The Right Worshipful the Mayor of the City of Bath
		The Worshipful the Mayor of the Royal Borough of Kingston upon Thames
		The Worshipful the Mayor of Colchester
LETTER		
Formal	*Begin*	Mr Mayor
	End	Yours faithfully
Social	*Begin*	Dear Mr Mayor
	End	Yours sincerely
Spoken		Mr Mayor, not Your Worship
		If the plural is required, it is acceptable to use 'Your Worships'

Mayoresses

Written

ENVELOPE		The Mayoress of Castleford
LETTER		
Formal	*Begin*	Madam Mayoress
	End	Yours faithfully
Social	*Begin*	Dear Mayoress
	End	Yours sincerely
Spoken		Mayoress

Aldermen

Although the office no longer exists in other parts of the country, the Corporation of London continues to appoint aldermen.

Written

ENVELOPE	Mr Alderman Parsons
	If a woman – Mrs or Miss Alderman
	If a knight – Alderman Sir Denis Petry
	If a peer – Alderman the Right Hon. Lord Lewes

If the alderman is a member of the armed forces his or her rank precedes the office.

LETTER

Formal	*Begin*	Dear Alderman
	End	Yours faithfully
Social	*Begin*	Dear Mr Parsons
	End	Yours sincerely
Spoken	Alderman Parsons or Alderman Mrs Young

Councillors

Written

| ENVELOPE | Councillor William Lawson |
| | or Councillor Mrs Hall |

LETTER

Formal	*Begin*	Dear Councillor Lawson
		or dear Councillor Mrs Hall
	End	Yours faithfully
Social	*Begin*	Dear Mr Lawson
	End	Yours sincerely
Spoken	Councillor Lawson
	or Councillor Mrs Hall

If a councillor has another rank or title, this should be used in preference to 'Councillor', unless council business is under discussion.

Municipal officers

In formal letters these should be addressed as 'Dear Sir'.
Otherwise they are addressed by their appointment, such as –
Dear Town Clerk.

Local government in Scotland

Lord provosts

In Aberdeen, Dundee, Edinburgh and Glasgow the district councils elect 'Lord Provosts'. The Lord Provost of Edinburgh takes the style 'The Right Hon.', and the Lord Provost of Glasgow 'The Right Hon. the Lord Provost of Glasgow'

Written
ENVELOPE	The Lord Provost of Dundee
LETTER	
Formal	*Begin* My Lord Provost
	End Yours faithfully
Social	*Begin* Dear Lord Provost
	End Yours sincerely
Spoken	My Lord Provost

Heads of other Scottish district councils are 'Provosts', 'Chairmen' and 'Convenors', who are addressed both formally and socially by their appointment –

Ernest Doubleday, Esq., Provost of Clydebank

7. The armed forces

As a general rule, male officers in all three services are addressed as 'Sir' by junior officers. Forms of address in the women's services are indicated on page 00.

The Royal Navy

Admiral of the fleet

The holder of this rank would almost certainly be titled and is addressed as such.

Written

ENVELOPE   Admiral of the Fleet the Earl of Essex, G.C.B.
LETTER
Formal   *Begin*   My Lord (if a peer)
                         or Sir
            End   Yours faithfully
Social   *Begin*   Dear Lord Essex
                         or Dear Admiral Grove
            End   Yours sincerely
Spoken   By title, although sometimes the naval rank is preferred. Socially he may be known as 'Admiral'.

The description in conversation would be according to title or by rank as 'the Admiral of the Fleet'.

Admirals, vice-admirals and rear-admirals

Although all these ranks may be addressed as 'Admiral', the exact title is always used on an envelope.

Written

ENVELOPE   Admiral Sir Gilbert MacMillan, G.B.E., D.S.O.
                 Vice-Admiral Sir Thomas Wainwright, G.C.B.
                 Rear-Admiral David Hyde, O.B.E.

LETTER		
Formal	*Begin*	Sir or Dear Sir
	End	Yours faithfully
Social	*Begin*	Dear Sir Gilbert
		or Dear Admiral Hyde
	End	Yours sincerely
Spoken		Sir Gilbert or Admiral Hyde

The description in conversation would be the same or, more informally, 'The Admiral'.

Commodores, captains

Officers below the rank of rear-admiral have the letters 'R.N.' or the words 'Royal Navy' following any decorations they may hold.

Written

ENVELOPE		Commodore Humphrey Beecham, O.B.E., Royal Navy
		Captain Raymond Perring, C.B.E., R.N.
LETTER		
Formal	*Begin*	Sir or Dear Sir
	End	Yours faithfully
Social	*Begin*	Dear Commodore Beecham
		Dear Captain Perring
	End	Yours sincerely
Spoken		Commodore Beecham or Captain Perring

Commanders, lieutenant-commanders

Written

ENVELOPE		Commander Joseph Unwin, M.B.E., Royal Navy
		Lieutenant-Commander Michael Swallow,
		O.B.E., R.N.
LETTER		
Formal	*Begin*	Sir or Dear Sir
	End	Yours faithfully
Social	*Begin*	Dear Commander Unwin
		Dear Commander Swallow
	End	Yours sincerely

Spoken   Commander Unwin or Commander Swallow
The exact rank is only used on the envelope.

Lieutenants

In speech lieutenants are formally addressed by their rank but
are socially referred to as 'Mr'. Sub-lieutenants and
midshipmen are addressed both formally and socially as 'Mr'.
Their ranks appear on envelopes as –

> Sub-Lieut. N.S. Grant, Royal Navy
> Midshipman L.R. Carroll, Royal Navy

Non-commissioned rates

A fleet chief petty officer is addressed as 'Mr' with his
surname at the beginning of a letter. Other rates are addressed
by rank, as follows –

> Petty Officer Haggard
> Able-bodied Seaman Thorne

Retired officers

Above the rank of lieutenant-commander an officer is usually
addressed by rank after retirement. An admiral of the fleet
remains on the active list throughout his life. The abbreviation
'Rtd.' only follows the name to prevent confusion (after
taking a civilian post, for example).

Titled officers

If a title is conferred on an officer, his naval rank precedes it,
for example –

> Commodore the Hon. Arnold Gibson, Royal Navy

Chaplains

Chaplains use their clerical title with the addition of the letters
'R.N.' after the name or following any decorations. The
chaplain of the fleet is an archdeacon and is therefore
addressed as 'The Venerable' with his name.

The Royal Marines

Officers in the Royal Marines are addressed in the same style as army officers (see The Army, below). 'R.M.' is added to the name if the rank is that of a lieutenant-colonel or below.

The Army

Field marshals

This rank is normally held by a peer, baronet or knight. It is held for life.

Written

ENVELOPE	Field Marshal the Lord Trevelyn, G.C.B., C.B.E.
	Field Marshal Sir Christopher Nell, K.C.B., C.B.E.
LETTER	

Formal	*Begin*	My Lord (if a peer)
		or Sir or Dear Sir
	End	Yours faithfully
Social	*Begin*	Dear Lord Trevelyn
		or Dear Sir Christopher
	End	Yours sincerely
Spoken		Either by title or military rank, whichever is preferred. He may be described in conversation as 'The Field Marshal'.

Generals, lieutenant-generals, major-generals

All these ranks are addressed as 'General'. The complete rank is only noted on envelopes and in a formal list.

Written

ENVELOPE	General Sir Thomas Trent, G.C.B., C.B.E., M.C.
	Major-General Charles Lee, O.B.E.
LETTER	

Formal	*Begin*	Sir or Dear Sir
	End	Yours faithfully
Social	*Begin*	Dear General Trent

End   Yours sincerely
Spoken   Sir Thomas (if a knight) or General Lee

Brigadiers

A brigadier is addressed as 'Brigadier' or 'Brigadier Bowles'.
Decorations and honours should follow the name on the
envelope or in a formal list.

Colonels, lieutenant-colonels

Both these ranks are addressed as 'Colonel', except on
envelopes and in formal lists, when the complete title is given.
The regiment may also be added if appropriate.

Majors, captains

These ranks are addressed as 'Major' or 'Captain'. The
regiment may also be shown on the envelope.

Lieutenants and second-lieutenants

Written
ENVELOPE   David Hyde, Esq.,
            Grenadier Guards
LETTER
Formal   *Begin*   Sir or Dear Sir
            End   Yours faithfully
Social   *Begin*   Dear Mr Hyde
            End   Yours sincerely
Spoken   Mr Hyde

Retired officers

As they are never technically retired, field marshals continue
to use their title for life. Other ranks above that of major may
choose to be addressed by their rank after retiring from the
active list. It is not common practice for ranks below major to
continue being addressed by rank.

Non-commissioned ranks

When writing abbreviated forms of ranks, full stops are not

required. The rank is never abbreviated at the beginning of a letter, for example –

> Dear Sergeant Major Woods
> Dear Corporal Bell
> Dear Gunner Morley

On envelopes the rank may be abbreviated and initials are used for forenames –

> CSM H. Leigh
> Cpl J.B. Cooke

In speech, a non-commissioned officer is addressed by rank with or without the surname. In the case of a private or the equivalent (sapper, rifleman, fusilier, etc.), the surname is always added –

> Rifleman Scott
> Fusilier MacPhie
> Gunner Bowen

The Royal Air Force

Marshals of the Royal Air Force

An officer of this rank remains on the active list for life.

Written		
ENVELOPE		Marshal of the Royal Air Force, Sir Dermot Porter, G.C.B., K.B.E., D.S.O.
LETTER		
Formal	*Begin*	My Lord (if a peer) or Sir or Dear Sir
	End	Yours faithfully
Social	*Begin*	Dear Lord Arden or Dear Sir Dermot (if a knight)
	End	Yours sincerely
Spoken		Lord Arden or Sir Dermot

Air chief marshals, air marshals, or air vice-marshals

The exact title is only used on an envelope and never in speech, when all of these ranks are addressed as 'Air Marshal'.

Air commodores, group captains, wing commanders, squadron leaders, flight lieutenants

Officers below and including the rank of air commodore take the letters 'R.A.F.' after their name and decorations. Their rank is used in full both in speech and writing. Flight lieutenants are always addressed in speech with their surname, for example –

> Flight Lieutenant Forbes

Flying officers, pilot officers

The rank may appear on an envelope as follows –

> Flying Officer Jeremy Manley, A.F.C., R.A.F.

However, in speech and at the beginning of letters the officer is styled 'Mr Manley'.

Chaplains

Chaplains are addressed by their clerical titles, whatever their rank within the service. The chaplain-in-chief is an archdeacon.

When the name of a chaplain is unknown, a letter may be addressed to –

> The Church of England Chaplain,
> R.A.F. Station,
> (followed by the address)

Retired officers

Officers above the rank of squadron leader may continue to use their title after retirement.

The Women's Services

The Women's Royal Navy Service

The letters 'W.R.N.S.' are added after the name and decorations of an officer.

Written
ENVELOPE   Second Officer G. Lyons, W.R.N.S.
LETTER
Formal   *Begin*   Dear Madam
                    or Dear Second Officer Lyons
          End   Yours faithfully
Social   *Begin*   Dear Second Officer Lyons
                    or Dear Miss Lyons
          End   Yours sincerely
Spoken   Second Officer Lyons

Junior officers address a senior officer as 'Ma'am'.

After retirement officers no longer use their rank.

In the non-commissioned rates a fleet chief wren is addressed as 'Miss' or 'Mrs' with her surname. Other rates are addressed by rank, for example –

> Leading Wren Grayson
> Chief Wren Armitage

The Women's Royal Army Corps

'W.R.A.C.' follows the name and decorations of an officer.

Written
ENVELOPE   Colonel B. Bradley, W.R.A.C.
LETTER
Formal   *Begin*   Dear Madam
                    or Dear Colonel Bradley
          End   Yours faithfully
Social   *Begin*   Dear Colonel Smith
          End   Yours sincerely

| *Spoken* | Lieutenants and second-lieutenants are addressed as 'Miss' or 'Mrs' with their surnames. Other officers are addressed by rank. |

Retired officers do not continue to use their service title.

In the non-commissioned ranks initials are used in preference to forenames, and the surname is followed by 'W.R.A.C.'

The Women's Royal Air Force

'W.R.A.F.' follows the name and decorations.

Written

ENVELOPE		Group Captain T. Wilkins, W.R.A.F.
LETTER		
Formal	*Begin*	Dear Madam
		or Dear Group Captain Wilkins
	End	Yours faithfully
Social	*Begin*	Dear Group Captain Wilkins
	End	Yours sincerely
Spoken		Group Captain Wilkins

After retirement officers do not continue using their service title.

8. The clergy

The Church of England

The Archbishops of Canterbury and of York

The Archbishop of Canterbury is Primate of all England and Metropolitan. The Archbishop of York is Primate of England and Metropolitan. Together with the Bishops of London, Durham and Winchester and twenty-one other bishops they form the Lords Spiritual in Parliament. They are both Privy Counsellors and are addressed on an envelope as such –

Written

ENVELOPE		The Most Reverend and Right Hon. the Lord Archbishop of Canterbury/York.
LETTER		
Formal	*Begin*	My Lord Archbishop
		or Dear Archbishop
	End	Yours faithfully
Social	*Begin*	Dear Archbishop
	End	Yours sincerely

Spoken

Formal	Your Grace
Social	Archbishop

In conversation, 'The Archbishop' is used, unless there is a possibility of confusion, when the territorial title would be used.

Other archbishops are addressed, on envelopes, as –

The Most Revd. the Lord Archbishop of ————
As a Privy Councillor the Bishop of London has the style –
Right Reverend and Right Honourable

The wife of an archbishop does not have a title, unless she or her husband has a temporal title.

The Primate of All Ireland

The Primate of All Ireland is the Archbishop of Armagh, who is addressed formally as –

The Most Revd. His Grace the Lord Primate of all Ireland. Other forms of address are as above.

Retired archbishops

Archbishops, on retirement, revert to the status of bishop. However, as a courtesy, he may still be addressed as an archbishop. It has been the custom for the Archbishop of Canterbury to receive a peerage on his retirement thus retaining his seat in the House of Lords. In speech, a retired archbishop is referred to by both his title and surname –

Archbishop Howell or Archbishop Lord Howell
'Bishop' may also be used, if preferred.

Bishops (England and Wales)

Diocesan bishops have traditionally taken the style of 'Lord Bishop', whether or not they qualify for membership of the House of Lords. Bishops suffragan, who are appointed to assist diocesan bishops, may also use this title, except in legal or official documents.

The forms of address for a bishop are –

Written

ENVELOPE	The Right Revd. the Lord Bishop of ———	
LETTER		
Formal	*Begin*	My Lord or My Lord Bishop
	End	Yours faithfully
Social	*Begin*	Dear Lord Bishop or Dear Bishop
	End	Yours sincerely

Spoken

Formal	My Lord
Social	Bishop

Wives of bishops are addressed simply as 'Mrs', unless their husband has a temporal title.

Irish bishops

As premier bishop of the Church of Ireland the Bishop of Meath is styled the 'Most Revd.' when addressed. In other instances the same rules apply as for English bishops.

Scottish bishops

As for English bishops, except for the Primus of Scotland who is addressed as 'My Lord Primus' or 'Primus'. He is addressed on an envelope as 'The Most Revd. the Primus'.

Retired bishops

After retirement bishops are addressed on envelopes by their names –

The Right Revd. David Brown

Sometimes a retired bishop may be appointed as an assistant to the bishop of the diocese in which he lives. He is still addressed by name, as above.

Deans

When used in the ecclesiastical rather than the academic sense, the title of 'Dean' denotes the head of a collegiate or cathedral church. He is addressed as follows –

Written

ENVELOPE		The Very Reverend the Dean of ————
LETTER		
Formal	*Begin*	Very Reverend Sir or Dear Sir
	End	Yours faithfully
Social	*Begin*	Dear Mr Dean or Dear Dean
	End	Yours sincerely

Spoken

Formal	Mr Dean or Dean
Social	Dean

In conversation he would be described as 'The Dean of ————'.

A retired dean is addressed as other clergy, unless he is appointed a 'Dean Emeritus'. This title is used only in official papers. The address on the envelope should include the personal name –

The Very Revd. John Davis, D.D.

Provosts

Where a cathedral has evolved from a parish church, a provost is usually appointed to it rather than a dean. Their roles are the same, and they are addressed as follows –

Written

ENVELOPE		The Very Reverend the Provost of ————
LETTER		
Formal	*Begin*	Very Reverend Sir or Dear Sir
	End	Yours faithfully
Social	*Begin*	Dear Provost or Dear Mr Provost
	End	Yours sincerely
Spoken		Mr Provost or Provost

The description in conversation would be 'The Provost (of ————)'.

A retired provost is addressed as other clergy.

Archdeacons

An archdeacon administers part of a diocese and supervises clergy. The word implies an office rather than a rank.

Written

ENVELOPE		The Venerable the Archdeacon of ————
LETTER		
Formal	*Begin*	Venerable Sir or Dear Sir (if not concerning Church matters)
	End	Yours faithfully
Social	*Begin*	Dear Archdeacon or Dear Mr Archdeacon
	End	Yours sincerely
Spoken		
Formal		Mr Archdeacon or Archdeacon
Social		Archdeacon

Description in conversation: The Archdeacon (of ———).

After retirement an archdeacon is addressed according to his rank in the clergy.

Canons

Whether a canon is honorary or residentiary the forms of address are the same.

Written

ENVELOPE	The Reverend Canon George Dyer	
LETTER		
Formal	*Begin*	Dear Canon or Dear Sir (if not concerning Church matters)
	End	Yours faithfully
Social	*Begin*	Dear Canon or Dear Canon Dyer
	End	Yours sincerely
Spoken	Canon or Canon Dyer	

Description in conversation: The Canon or Canon Dyer.

A retired canon is addressed as other clergy. An honorary canon retains his title, unless he leaves the Church or resigns it officially.

Prebendaries

A prebendary is a member of the chapter of certain cathedrals. The forms of address are –

Written

ENVELOPE	The Reverend Prebendary Ernest Lowe	
LETTER		
Formal	*Begin*	Reverend Sir or Dear Sir
	End	Yours faithfully
Social	*Begin*	Dear Prebendary or Dear Prebendary Lowe
	End	Yours sincerely
Spoken	Prebendary or Prebendary Smith	

After retirement a prebendary is addressed as other clergy.

Other clergy

When addressing clergy, initials or the personal name should always be mentioned. It is an American custom to style a clergyman 'The Reverend Dobson' or 'Reverend Dobson'; it is not generally accepted in Britain, unless the name or initial is unknown.

Written

ENVELOPE   The Reverend Charles Dobson
LETTER
Formal   *Begin*   Reverend Sir; Sir
                 End   Yours faithfully
Social   *Begin*   Dear Sir; Dear Vicar; Dear Rector
                 End   Yours sincerely
Spoken   Mr Dobson

The description in conversation would be 'Mr Dobson', 'The Vicar' or 'The Rector'.

If the clergyman has a doctor's degree he may be styled 'Dr Dobson'.

Titled clerics

Where the priest has a title, the spiritual title always precedes the temporal, for example –

            The Revd. The Hon. Barnaby Spencer

Although knighthoods are not bestowed on priests in Holy Orders, it is possible for them to be appointed to an order of knighthood without use of the title. The abbreviation would follow the name in this case –

            The Right Revd. Barnaby Spencer, K.C.V.O.

Anglican religious communities (men)

Ordained members of religious communities are addressed as 'Father', and lay members as 'Brother'. The Order of St Francis is an exception to this, as all members of that community are styled 'Brother'. Benedictine monks may all use the style 'Dom'. Most religious communities have letters which follow the name (see Appendix 2, Religious orders).

The head of each religious order is addressed by his office both in the written and the spoken form –

> Father Abbot
> Father Prior
> Father Superior

In conversation, he is described as 'The Abbott', etc.

For other ordained and lay members the forms of address are as follows –

Written

ENVELOPE	The Reverend George Lawson, C.R.
	The Reverend Dom James Scott, O.S.B.
	(Benedictine)
	Brother Michael, S.S.F. (Franciscan)
LETTER	
Begin	All ordained members may be addressed as –
	Dear Reverend Father
	Alternatively the name may be used –
	Dear Brother Michael
End	Yours sincerely
Spoken	Father George or Father George Lawson
	Dom James or Father Scott
	Brother Michael

Where confusion might occur the surname may be used.

Anglican religious communities (women)

Superiors are addressed as follows –
Written

ENVELOPE	The Reverend Mother Superior
	The Reverend the Prioress
	The Right Reverend the Lady Abbess
LETTER	
Begin	Dear Mother Superior
	Dear Prioress
	Dear Lady Abbess

End	Yours sincerely
Spoken	Reverend Mother
	Mother Prioress
	Lady Abbess or Mother Abbess

Other members of the community are known as 'Mother' or 'Sister', according to the custom, followed by their forenames and surnames. The initials of the order follow the name.

Chaplains

See Chapter 7.

Chancellors

The 'Diocesan Chancellor' advises the bishop on legal matters and acts as judge in episcopal courts.

Written

ENVELOPE	The Reverend Chancellor Matthew Wright
	or The Worshipful Chancellor Matthew Wright
LETTER	
Formal	*Begin* Dear Mr Chancellor or Dear Sir
	End Yours faithfully
Social	*Begin* Dear Chancellor
	End Yours sincerely

Spoken

Formal	Mr Chancellor
Social	Chancellor
In court	Sir or Worshipful Sir

If the office is held by a woman she is styled 'Madam Chancellor' or 'Chancellor'. In court she is addressed as 'Worshipful Madam'.

The Free Churches

Methodist and Baptist Churches

The Presidents of the Methodist Church and the Baptist
Church of Great Britain are addressed on the platform as 'Mr
President'. A deaconess of the Methodist Church is addressed
as 'Sister', followed by her full name. In the written address
she is referred to as 'Deaconess', followed by her full name.
 Ministers are addressed as follows –

Written

ENVELOPE		The Reverend Henry Thomas
		The Reverend Valerie Glenn
LETTER		
Formal	*Begin*	Dear Sir or Dear Minister or Dear Madam
	End	Yours faithfully
Social	*Begin*	Dear Mr Thomas
	End	Yours sincerely
Spoken		Mr Thomas. If the minister holds a doctor's degree 'Dr Thomas' would be used.

United Reform Church

The Moderator of the General Assembly of the United
Reform Church is referred to as 'Moderator' or 'Mr
Moderator' in written and verbal forms of address. The
envelope is addressed –

 The Rt. Rev. Andrew Nelson.

The Salvation Army

Officers are addressed according to their rank, for example
'Dear Major'. Married women take their husband's rank on
marriage, such as 'Mrs Major Gerald Jones'.

The Church of Scotland

The Lord High Commissioner to the General Assembly

The same form of address is used whether the office is held by
a man or woman or whether it is a member of the royal
family. The only exception to this would be the Duke of
Edinburgh, who would be addressed as 'Royal Highness'.

Written

ENVELOPE		His (or Her) Grace the Lord High Commissioner
LETTER		
Formal	*Begin*	Your Grace
and social	*End*	I have the honour to remain, Your Grace's most devoted and obedient servant

Spoken   Your Grace

The description in conversation would be 'The Lord High
Commissioner'.

The Moderator of the General Assembly

Written

ENVELOPE		The Right Rev. the Moderator of the General Assembly of the Church of Scotland
LETTER		
Formal	*Begin*	Dear Sir or Dear Moderator
	End	Yours faithfully
Social	*Begin*	Dear Mr (or Doctor) Jenkins or Dear Moderator
	End	Yours sincerely

Spoken

Formal and social   Moderator

The office is held for one year. Thereafter the former
moderator is styled 'The Very Reverend Arthur Jenkins'.

Dean of the Chapel Royal and Dean of the Thistle

These are addressed in the same manner as a dean of the
Church of England.

Other Clergy

The titles 'Vicar' or 'Rector' are not used. The parish minister
or the minister is styled 'The Minister of ————' on an
envelope.

The Roman Catholic Church

The territorial titles described below are used within the
Roman Catholic Church and unofficially. Official documents
do not employ them as they have no basis in law.

The Pope

Written

ENVELOPE	His Holiness The Pope	
LETTER		
Formal	*Begin*	Your Holiness or Most Holy Father
	End	For Roman Catholics –
		I have the honour to be
		Your Holiness's most devoted and
		obedient child
		For non-Catholics –
		I have the honour to be
		Your Holiness's obedient servant

Spoken   Your Holiness

The Pope is described in conversation as 'His Holiness' or
'The Pope'.

Cardinals

Written

ENVELOPE	His Eminence Cardinal Mahon	
LETTER		
Formal	*Begin*	Your Eminence (recognised officially)
		or My Lord Cardinal
	End	For Roman Catholics –
		I have the honour to be,
		My Lord Cardinal,

		Your Eminence's devoted and obedient child.
		For non-Catholics –
		I remain,
		Your Eminence,
		Yours faithfully
Social	*Begin*	Dear Cardinal
	End	Yours sincerely

Spoken

| Formal | Your Eminence |
| Social | Cardinal (Mahon) |

Cardinals who are archbishops or bishops would be addressed on an envelope as 'His Eminence Cardinal Mahon, Archbishop (or Bishop) of ——————'.

Archbishops

Written

ENVELOPE	His Grace the Archbishop of Liverpool or The Most Reverend Archbishop Fitzgerald
LETTER	
Formal	*Begin*	My Lord Archbishop or Most Reverend Sir
	End	I have the honour to be, Most Reverend Sir, Your obedient servant or Yours faithfully
Social	*Begin*	Dear Archbishop
	End	Yours sincerely

Spoken

| Formal | Your Grace |
| Social | Archbishop |

Bishops

Written

ENVELOPE	The Right Revd. Bishop Wheelan
LETTER	
Formal	*Begin*	My Lord or Right Reverend Sir (Most Reverend in Ireland)

68

	End	I remain,
		My Lord,
		Yours faithfully
		or I have the honour to be,
		Right Reverend Sir,
		Your obedient servant
Social	*Begin*	Dear Bishop or Dear Bishop Wheelan
	End	Yours sincerely

Spoken

Formal	My Lord
Social	Bishop

Retired bishops are given the honorary title of a diocese no longer in use. They are addressed by name and the titular see is not included on the envelope.

Monsignorl

Written

ENVELOPE	The Reverend Monsignor Patrick Hanley
	or The Reverend Monsignor

LETTER

Formal	*Begin*	Reverend Sir
	End	Yours faithfully
Social	*Begin*	Dear Monsignor Hanley
	End	Yours sincerely

Spoken   Monsignor Hanley

Canons

Written

ENVELOPE	The Very Revd. Canon Stephen Turner

LETTER

Formal	*Begin*	Very Reverend Sir or Dear Sir
	End	Yours faithfully
Social	*Begin*	Dear Canon Turner or Dear Canon
	End	Yours sincerely

Spoken   Canon Turner

Abbots

Written

ENVELOPE   The Right Reverend, the Abbot of Wendale
(followed by the initials of his order)
or The Right Reverend Bernard Ward
(followed by the initials of his order)

LETTER

Formal	*Begin*	My Lord Abbot or Right Reverend Sir
	End	I beg to remain, my Lord Abbot,
		Your devoted and obedient servant
		or Yours faithfully
Social	*Begin*	Dear Father Abbot
	End	Yours sincerely

Spoken

Formal	Father Abbot
Social	Abbot

Provincials

Written

ENVELOPE   The Very Revd. Father Provincial

LETTER

Formal	*Begin*	Very Reverend Father Provincial
	End	Yours faithfully
Social	*Begin*	Dear Father or Dear Father Provincial
	End	Yours sincerely

Spoken   Father Provincial

Priests

Written

ENVELOPE   The Reverend Michael Brown
or The Revd. Father Brown

LETTER

Formal	*Begin*	Dear Reverend Father
	End	Yours faithfully
Social	*Begin*	Dear Father Brown
	End	Yours sincerely

Spoken   Father, or Father Brown where there may be
             confusion or on introduction.

Religious communities (men)

Both clerics and lay monks of the Order of St Benedict are
styled 'Dom'. The letters 'O.S.B.' may be added after the
name on the envelope. Monks preparing for the priesthood, or
those who have not taken final vows, are called 'Brothers'.
The head of the Benedictine order in Great Britain is the
'Abbot President'.

The members of some religious communities are called
'Friars' rather than monks. These include the Dominicans,
Augustinians, Carmelites and Franciscans.

Religious communities (women)

Heads of communities are addressed by title, for example –

> The Lady Abbess
> The Reverend Mother
> The Sister Superior
> The Mother Prioress

It is becoming more common for a nun to be addressed by her
own full name ('Sister ————') rather than by an adopted
religious name. The appropriate letters for an order are placed
after the name. Benedictine nuns may formally be styled
'Dame', although 'Sister' is used in everyday language.

The Jewish community

The Chief Rabbi

Written
ENVELOPE   The Chief Rabbi Dr David Cohen
             or The Very Revd. the Chief Rabbi
LETTER
Formal   *Begin* Dear Chief Rabbi or Dear Sir
             End   Yours faithfully

Social	*Begin*	Dear Chief Rabbi
	End	Yours sincerely
Spoken	Chief Rabbi	

Rabbis

Written

ENVELOPE	Rabbi Julia Stein	
	or Rabbi Dr David Cohen	
LETTER		
Formal	*Begin*	Dear Sir/Madam
	End	Yours faithfully
Social	*Begin*	Dear Rabbi Stein
	End	Yours sincerely
Spoken	Rabbi Stein or Dr Cohen	

Ministers

Written

ENVELOPE	The Reverend Immanuel Goldstein	
LETTER		
Formal	*Begin*	Dear Sir or Reverend Sir
	End	Yours faithfully
Social	*Begin*	Dear Mr Goldstein
	End	Yours sincerely
Spoken	Mr Goldstein or Dr Goldstein (if a doctor)	

Readers and cantors are also styled 'The Reverend'.

9. Royalty

The sovereign

The prospect of meeting the queen is one which worries many people. Royal visits to factories, schools and civic functions are carefully supervised by palace officials and advice is given as to protocol. Presentations to royalty certainly should not be an ordeal, especially if a few simple rules are remembered.

When the queen enters a room it is the custom for the women to curtsey and the men to bow. This is repeated when a personal introduction is made. The curtsey should not be too deep and the bow from the neck only. It is correct to touch the queen's extended hand at the same time. This should be light and not a firm handshake. Men and women in uniform may salute, if this is appropriate to their service. Men should remove their gloves when shaking hands, but women may retain theirs as long as the queen is wearing gloves also. The sovereign should always initiate any conversation. At the end of it a second curtsey or bow should be made together with a slight movement backwards.

Forms of address in writing and speech are as follows –

Written

ENVELOPE   All correspondence to the queen is addressed to – 'The Private Secretary to Her Majesty The Queen'.

Further correspondence should be addressed by name to the person who replies.

LETTER

Formal   *Begin*   Dear Sir/Madam

The letter should ask the private secretary to 'direct Her Majesty's attention to . . .' the matter contained. Otherwise it might suggest that 'it may interest Her Majesty to know . . .' Following the first reference to 'Her Majesty', other references may be to 'The Queen'.

	End	Yours faithfully
Social		If the writer is known to the queen, or if direct communication is required the letter begins –
		Madam,
		or May it please Your Majesty
	End	I have the honour to remain, Madam, Your Majesty's most humble and obedient servant
		or Madam,
		with my humble duty,

Such letters are no longer written in the third person.

| *Spoken* | 'Your Majesty' at first. Thereafter 'Ma'am' (to rhyme with jam). |

The queen is described in conversation as 'Her Majesty' or 'The Queen'.

When introducing another person to the queen, the correct form is – 'May I present Julian Field, Your Majesty?'

A speech at an official function at which the queen is present should begin 'May it please Your Majesty'. Later references should be to 'Your Majesty' or 'Ma'am'.

The royal family

The Queen Mother

The same forms of address apply as for the queen. The envelope in any direct communication would read –

To Her Majesty Queen Elizabeth the Queen Mother

The Duke of Edinburgh

The Duke of Edinburgh is styled as a royal prince.

Royal princes and princesses

When being introduced to a royal prince or princess it is the custom to bow or curtsey. As they will have their own household, most correspondence is addressed to the private secretary or lady-in-waiting. Children of the sovereign take

'The' before their name.

Written

ENVELOPE | The Private Secretary to The Prince Andrew
LETTER

Formal   *Begin*   Dear Sir/Madam

The first reference to the prince or princess in the letter should be to 'His/Her Royal Highness'. Thereafter 'Prince' or 'Princess' is used.

               End   Yours faithfully

Social | If the writer is known to the prince or princess, direct communication would be as follows –

ENVELOPE | His Royal Highness,
           The Prince Edward
           End of I have the honour to be,
           letter   Sir/Madam,
                  Your Royal Highness's most humble and obedient servant

Spoken | 'Your Royal Highness' at first. Thereafter 'Sir' or 'Ma'am'.

Other members of the royal family

Apart from those mentioned above, members of the royal family who are not peers are styled according to their branch of the family, for example –

     His Royal Highness Prince Michael of Kent

His wife also takes her husband's style, for example –

     Her Royal Highness Princess Michael of Kent

When introducing someone to a member of the royal family, the correct form is 'May I present Derek Forsyth, Your Royal Highness?'

A married princess is addressed on envelopes and invitations with her husband's title, for example –

Her Royal Highness Princess Alexandra, the Hon. Mrs Angus Ogilvy.

Her Royal Highness Princess Anne, Mrs Mark Phillips

Members of royal households

Ladies-in-waiting are appointed to the queen and the queen mother and to all lady members of the royal family who are styled 'Royal Highness'.

The head of the queen's household is the 'Lord Chamberlain'. He is responsible for all state and ceremonial functions. The 'Lord Steward' takes charge of domestic arrangements, especially state banquets, and the 'Master of the Horse' looks after the queen's safety. In addition to these offices, other responsibilities are undertaken by –

Lords-in-waiting: these are appointed by the government and represent the queen at memorial services and other important occasions when the sovereign is unable to attend.

The Vice-Chamberlain: this office is held by an M.P. who informs the sovereign about parliamentary business.

The Crown Equerry: he takes charge of the royal travelling arrangements.

The Master of the Household: he is responsible for the day-to-day running of the queen's household.

The Keeper of the Privy Purse: he acts as a treasurer, with responsibility for finance.

The Private Secretary and the Press Secretary: these act as coordinators handling communications with the public and replies to individual enquiries, as well as relations with the press.

Members of royal households are addressed according to their own rank. If this is not known, it is acceptable to address them by office, for example –

The Private Secretary to ————

Other members of the Royal Family also have their own households. Letters to any of these should be addressed to the private secretary. Correspondence with Princess Alexandra is dealt with by her lady-in-waiting.

10. The peerage: from dukes to barons

The peerage may be divided into five grades. They are, in descending order, dukes, marquesses, earls, viscounts and barons. Within each grade there are some variations which will be dealt with in the relevant section. The peerage has the most complicated and diverse of all forms of address, and they have been simplified wherever possible.

Dukes and duchesses

The title of a duke is always taken from the name of a place.

Written

ENVELOPE   His Grace the Duke of Essex
           Her Grace the Duchess of Essex

LETTER

Formal   *Begin*   My Lord Duke
                     Madam or Dear Madam
           End   Yours faithfully
Social   *Begin*   Dear Duke
                     Dear Duchess
           End   Yours sincerely

Spoken

Formal   Your Grace
Social   Duke
           Duchess

If only one duke is present the description in conversation is 'the Duke'. Otherwise the placename is mentioned – 'The Duke of Essex'. A duke or duchess is entitled to the prefix 'The Most Noble . . .', but this is rarely used except on some official documents.

Elder sons of dukes

The eldest son of a duke has his title from birth. He normally uses the highest of his father's other titles as a 'courtesy title'. For example, the eldest son of the Duke of Devonshire would take the title Marquess of Hartington. On his marriage his wife would take the title Marchioness of Hartington. His eldest son would take the third title of the Duke of Devonshire, Earl of Burlington. Following the death of a peer, the heir is addressed by his courtesy title until after the funeral.

The holder of the courtesy title of 'Marquess' is not styled 'The Most Hon'. Nor is an earl, viscount or baron, by courtesy, addressed as 'The Right Hon.'. In correspondence, 'The' is omitted before the title. In the event of the death of the eldest son, his courtesy title may pass to his son.

Daughters and younger sons of dukes

The daughters and the younger sons of a duke would be styled 'Lord' or 'Lady' with their first and family names –
> Lord Nicholas Green
> Lady Emma Green

If the title is shortened, only the forename is used –
> Lord Nicholas
> Lady Emma

It is incorrect to use the family name, such as 'Lord Green'.

Wives of younger sons of dukes

The wife of a younger son of a duke is addressed as 'Lady Nicholas Green' or 'Lady Nicholas' – never as 'Lady Green'.

Former wives and widows of dukes

Former wives and widows do not keep the title if they remarry.

Children of younger sons and daughters of dukes

The children of a duke's younger sons or daughters do not bear a title.

When a daughter of a duke marries she keeps her title, unless her husband is a peer, in which case she takes her husband's title. If she marries a commoner, she may retain her title whilst taking her husband's surname. Lady Emma Green, following her marriage to Mr Clive Jamieson, would become Lady Emma Jamieson.

Other ranks of the peerage

Except when addressed on envelopes, in invitations and at very formal functions, a marquess, earl or viscount is not referred to by his exact title but is called 'Lord ————'. A baron is addressed by his exact title only in formal documents. At all other times he is know as 'Lord ————'.

Marquesses and Marchionesses

Written
ENVELOPE
Formal   The Most Hon. the Marquess of Shropshire
             The Most Hon. The Marchioness of Shropshire
Social   The Marquess of Shropshire
             The Marchioness of Shropshire
LETTER
Formal   *Begin*   My Lord
                       Madam
             End   Yours faithfully
Social   *Begin*   Dear Lord Shropshire
                       Dear Lady Shropshire
             End   Yours sincerely

Armed forces rank or ecclesiastical or ambassadorial titles precede a peer's rank in correspondence, for example –
             General the Lord Shropshire

Spoken
Formal   My Lord
Social   Lord Shropshire

In conversation, the marquess would be described as 'Lord

Shropshire' and the marchioness as 'Lady Shropshire'. The form of address used by employees would be 'His Lordship' or 'Her Ladyship'. Unless it is necessary for some reason, the exact rank of a peer would not be mentioned in speech.

Earls and countesses

Written
ENVELOPE

Formal	The Right Hon. the Earl of Grantham
	The Right Hon. the Countess of Grantham
Social	The Earl of Grantham
	The Countess of Grantham

LETTER

Formal	*Begin*	My Lord
		Madam
	End	Yours faithfully
Social	*Begin*	Dear Lord Grantham
		Dear Lady Grantham
	End	Yours sincerely

Spoken

Formal	My Lord
	Madam
Social	Lord Grantham
	Lady Grantham

Viscounts and viscountesses

This title is usually written with the omission of the preposition 'of', even if the name is territorial. Viscount Cobham, for example, is not styled 'Viscount of Cobham'.

Written
ENVELOPE

Formal	The Right Hon. the Viscount Tonbridge
	The Right Hon. the Viscountess Tonbridge
Social	The Viscount Tonbridge
	The Viscountess Tonbridge

Formal	*Begin*	My Lord
		Madam
	End	Yours faithfully
Social	*Begin*	Dear Lord Tonbridge
		Dear Lady Tonbridge
	End	Yours sincerely
Spoken		Lord Tonbridge
		Lady Tonbridge

Barons and baronesses

The wife of a baron is addressed as 'Lady ————'. If, however, the baroness is a peer in her own right, she may prefer to use the style 'Baroness ————' (see Peeresses in their own right, below).

Written
ENVELOPE

Formal	The Right Hon. Lord Rochester
	The Right Hon. Lady Rochester
Social	The Lord Rochester
	The Lady Rochester

LETTER

Formal	*Begin*	My Lord
		Madam
	End	Yours faithfully
Social	*Begin*	Dear Lord Rochester
		Dear Lady Rochester
	End	Yours sincerely
Spoken		Lord Rochester
		Lady Rochester

Peeresses in their own right

A peeress in her own right is addressed as the wife of a peer for the equivalent grade of the peerage – that is, marchioness, countess, viscountess. A baroness may also be styled 'Lady ————', according to her preference. Both these titles should be accompanied by the family or territorial name –

The Baroness Elgin
The Lady Murrey

Dowagers

A dowager is the earliest surviving widow of a peer. She may
be known, for example, as 'The Dowager Duchess of Sussex'.
Many holders of such a title prefer to be known by their first
name. If the present duke is unmarried, the widow may simply
be known as 'The Duchess of Sussex'. Should the present
duke marry, it is the custom for the widow to announce the
style by which she would prefer to be known.

Other widows of the same peer would be addressed by
their first name and title –

Gwendoline, Duchess of Sussex

If a peeress remarries, the title is no longer used, unless she is
a peeress in her own right. Former wives of peers use their
forenames together with the title, but are no longer addressed
as 'Your Grace'.

Honourables

The eldest sons of both viscounts and barons do not take
courtesy titles from their fathers. They are addressed in the
same fashion as their brothers and sisters as 'The Honourable
————'. or 'The Hon.' in written communications. If, for
example, the family name of Baron Rochester is Cochrane, the
eldest son would be known as –

The Honourable David Cochrane

His wife is styled –

The Hon. Mrs David Cochrane

The prefix should never be used in speech, when the couple
would be addressed as –

Mr and Mrs David Cochrane

Daughters of viscounts and barons are addressed in
writing as –

The Hon. Sylvia Crombie

Following her marriage, the daughter would take her husband's name but keep the title –

The Hon. Mrs Quentin Fortescue

In speech, the title is dropped, and the address would be 'Miss Crombie' or 'Mrs Fortescue'

The grandchildren of viscounts and barons have no title.

The younger sons of earls also take the title of 'The Honourable' before their name.

Life peers and peeresses

The form of address for a life peer is the same as that for an hereditary peer. Their children may bear a courtesy title for life.

Disclaimed peerages

Since 1963 it has been possible to disclaim an hereditary peerage in the United Kingdom. It is not possible to disclaim a life peerage. Once a peerage has been disclaimed, the peer reverts to his previous status. Courtesy titles deriving from the peerage may not be used, but a knighthood or baronetcy may be retained.

The wife of a disclaimed peer reverts to the same style as her husband, although the children may choose to keep any courtesy titles which they may have had previously.

Scottish peers

There are no barons in the Scottish peerage. The Scottish equivalent of this rank is a 'Lord of Parliament'.

The title of 'Master' is applicable to the heir apparent of a peer or a peeress in her own right, and to his son and heir. It is also the style adopted by the next in line to the peer or peeress in her own right (the heir presumptive). The heir apparent to a duke, marquess or earl uses his courtesy title rather than 'Master'. The heir apparent to a viscount or a lord, however, will be known by this title.

Written

ENVELOPE	The Master of Glenroe	
LETTER		
Formal	*Begin*	Sir or Dear Sir
	End	Yours faithfully
Social	*Begin*	Dear Master of Glenroe
	End	Yours sincerely

Spoken

Formal and social	Master

In conversation, within the household, the description is 'The Master'. Formally he is referred to as 'Sir'. On social occasions he may be addressed by his surname, for example –

Mr MacMillan

The wife of a master is addressed in correspondence as –

The Hon. Mrs MacMillan of Glenroe

otherwise as 'Mrs MacMillan'.

11. Baronets, knights and other titles

Baronets

The title of 'Baronet' is hereditary and is distinguished from a knighthood by the addition of the abbreviation 'Bt.' after the name.

Written

ENVELOPE   Sir William Peters, Bt.

LETTER

Formal	*Begin*	Sir or Dear Sir
	End	Yours faithfully
Social	*Begin*	Dear Sir William
	End	Yours sincerely

Spoken

Formal and social   Sir William

The only baronetcies which may be held by a woman are Scottish. The address on an envelope would carry the following abbreviation –

Lady Campbell of Kinross, Btss.

Wives of Baronets

Although the old-fashioned form of address 'Dame' may be used on legal documents, it is more usual for the wife of a baronet to be styled 'Lady'. This is used before the surname, unless there is the possibility of confusion, when the husband's forename may be added.

If a baronet's wife is the daughter of a viscount or a baron, 'The Honourable Lady ————' is the correct form. Daughters of earls, marquesses and dukes take the prefix 'Lady' before their name.

Written

Widows of baronets

Although the widow of a baronet may be officially styled the
'Dowager Lady Peters', it is more likely that she would wish
to use her forename –

Helen, Lady Peters

Otherwise, the forms of address are the same as those for the
wife of a baronet. If the widow remarries, she takes the style
of her new husband.

Former wives of baronets are addressed as 'Marion, Lady
Peters', unless they remarry.

Children of a baronet

The children of a baronet do not have any special style.
Adopted children do not have the right of succession.

Knights and dames

Knighthoods are only held for life. As soon as the knighthood
is announced, the recipient may use the prefix 'Sir' together
with one forename and the surname. The sovereign may
confer one of two kinds of knighthood. These are knighthoods
of an order of chivalry or the title of 'Knight Bachelor'.

Orders of chivalry carry their own precedence. The most
senior of these are the Order of the Garter and the Order of

the Thistle. Knights of these orders are distinguished by the letters which follow their names –

> The Duke of Norfolk, K.G.
> The Earl of Selkirk, K.T.

In both instances it is usual for the honours to be conferred on peers or Scottish nobles.

Other orders of chivalry are divided into classes. The Most Noble Order of the Bath, for example, is divided as follows –

Men

Knights Grand Cross	Sir Terence Woburn, G.C.B.
Knights Commanders	Sir Reginald Gower, K.C.B.
Companions	Stephen Maine, Esq., C.B.

Women

Dames Grand Cross	Dame Natasha Collins, G.C.B.
Dames Commanders	Dame Vera Wolsey, D.C.B.
Companions	Mrs Browning, C.B.

Forms of address for knights are as follows –

Written

ENVELOPE		Sir Terence Woburn, G.C.B.
LETTER		
Formal	*Begin*	Sir or Dear Sir
	End	Yours faithfully
Social	*Begin*	Dear Sir Terence
	End	Yours sincerely

Spoken

Formal and social	Sir Terence

Clergy with knighthoods

A member of the clergy of the Church of England who receives a knighthood uses the relevant letters after his name but only his clerical title as a prefix, for example –

> The Rt. Revd. the Lord Bishop of Castleford, K.C.B.

Honorary knighthoods

Occasionally, a foreign national may receive an honorary knighthood. In this instance the appropriate letters would be placed after the name, but 'Sir' is not used.

Dames

A dame is addressed in the following manner –

Written

ENVELOPE   Dame Muriel Peach, D.C.B.

LETTER

Formal	*Begin*	Madam or Dear Madam
	End	Yours faithfully
Social	*Begin*	Dear Dame Muriel
	End	Yours sincerely

Spoken

Formal and social   Dame Muriel

If the holder also has a higher title, 'Sir' or 'Dame' are disregarded as a prefix and only the letters after the name are used. 'The Hon.' may be used together with either prefix and should precede them –

The Hon. Dame Clara Selfridge, D.C.B.

The children of knights and dames are not accorded any special title.

Other orders of knighthood

The Royal Victorian Order has five classes which are applicable to both men and women. Only the first two classes entitle the holder to the style 'Sir' or 'Dame'.

Men

Knights Grand Cross	Sir Herbert Gibson, G.C.V.O.
Knights Commanders	Sir Charles Lyons, K.C.V.O.
Commanders	Nigel Vaughan, Esq., C.V.O.
Members Fourth Class	Quentin Fox, Esq., M.V.O.
Members Fifth Class	Richard Pembroke, Esq., M.V.O.

Women

Dames Grand Cross	Dame Cecily Hastings, G.C.V.O.
Dames Commanders	Dame Maureen Wilson, D.C.V.O.
Commanders	Miss Taylor, C.V.O.
Members Fourth Class	Mrs Hume, M.V.O.
Members Fifth Class	Miss Beck, M.V.O.

The Most Excellent Order of the British Empire is also divided into classes. The first three are the same as those of The Royal Victorian Order, using the letters G.B.E., K.B.E. and C.B.E. for men, and G.B.E., D.B.E. and C.B.E. for women. The fourth class is that of 'Officer' (O.B.E.) and the fifth 'Member' (M.B.E.).

The abbreviations for other orders of knighthood and the order in which they are written are described in the appendix.

Knights bachelor

The form of address for a knight bachelor is the simplest of all as it carries no letters after the name. The forename and surname is preceded by 'Sir', for example –

Sir Thomas Field

In some legal documents 'Knight' may be added, but neither this nor the abbreviation 'Kt' is used at any other time.

Wives of knights bachelor

The wife of a knight has the same style as the wife of a baronet, unless her husband is a Church of England clergyman. In this case, she would be addressed as Mrs Cecil Roberts, unless she has a title in her own right.

Widows of knights

The widow of a knight continues to use her title after the death of her husband, unless she remarries.

Multiple honours

If a knight is the recipient of more than one order of knighthood, these are placed in order of precedence after his name. If there are also different classes, the higher class will take precedence even if it is of a lower order. All the relevant letters should be included, and never be amended to 'etc.'.

Scottish titles

Chiefs of clans and names

'Mr' is not used when addressing a Scottish chief of clan. Chiefs of 'whole' names or clans are addressed as follows –

Written

ENVELOPE   The Mackintosh of Mackintosh
                or Macpherson of Cluny

Knights are distinguished by the prefix 'Sir' –
                Sir Jean Dunbar of Mochrum

LETTER

Formal   *Begin*   Sir or Dear Sir
                    Another clansman begins 'Dear Chief'.
        End   Yours faithfully

Social   *Begin*   Dear Mackintosh or Dear Cluny
        End   Yours sincerely

Spoken   Mackintosh or Macpherson

Wives of chiefs

The wife of a chief of clan or name takes her husband's style with the addition of 'Mrs' –

         Mrs Mackintosh of Mackintosh
         or Mrs Macpherson of Cluny

Widows of chiefs

The widow of a chief of clan is styled –

         The Dowager Mrs Mackintosh of Mackintosh

Heirs of Chiefs

The heir to a chief of clan is described as –

         Donald Mackintosh, Younger of Mackintosh

12. Family matters

What's in a name?

Addressing people by their correct name is fundamental to good manners but is not always easy. Never be afraid to ask if you do not catch someone's name when it is first spoken. Most people with unusual names are used to being addressed incorrectly and will be glad to help. It is better to take the trouble to find out than mumble the name or omit it totally.

Whether you use the forename or the surname of an individual depends on your relationship with him or her. In certain circumstances you should not use a first name without having been invited to do so. This would normally be the case with someone who is senior to you in age (such as your girlfriend's mother) or status (for example, your employer). Much will depend on the general atmosphere of a situation. In some families and occupations there is a greater degree of formality than in others. Public-school habits die hard, and grown men may still be heard calling each other by their surnames only. If in doubt it would be as well to ask someone quietly how a person is usually addressed rather than presuming that you can call them what you like.

Introductions

It is not a good idea to follow an introduction to your friend's Aunt Edwina with the words, 'Do you mind if I call you Edwina?' She may mind a great deal but would hardly be likely to reply, 'Yes, I do, actually'.

When introducing one person to another it is usual to introduce the younger or junior person to the elder or senior person. Unless the woman is much younger than a man, it is better to introduce a man to a woman. It helps to put people at their ease if some information is added to an introduction. For example, 'Mrs Watson, I would like you to meet my brother Norman. He and his wife will shortly be moving into this area'.

Mr, Mrs, Miss and Ms

All the above are prefixes and should not be regarded as part
of a name. Attaching them to a name denotes the sex or
marital status of a person, and such prefixes should not be
used unless they accompany a name. Signatures are always
written without the use of a prefix, although women may add
Miss, Mrs or Ms in brackets afterwards to indicate the style
by which they prefer to be addressed –

> Yours sincerely,
>
> *Catherine Blake*
>
> Catherine Blake (Ms)

If a letter is signed in this way, the return envelope should
include the prefix –

Ms Catherine Blake

If a prefix has not been added, it is correct to address the
person by both the forename and surname –

Catherine Blake

After marriage it is usual for a woman to adopt her
husband's name. It should be remembered that, although she
may sign herself Marcia Dormer, she should be addressed in
correspondence as –

Mrs Henry Dormer or Mrs H.K. Dormer

Traditionally, the wife of the head of a family may be
known simply as 'Mrs Bradshaw', and other married women
in the same family by the addition of their husband's
forename, for example, 'Mrs George Bradshaw'. This is simply
to identify the different generations which may exist within
one family, but it is not always observed.

Similarly, where there are several unmarried daughters, the eldest may be styled 'Miss Bradshaw' and the younger members addressed as 'Miss Jane Bradshaw', 'Miss Pamela Bradshaw', and so on.

'Ms' (pronounced Mizz) may be used in addressing a married or unmarried woman, but it is advisable to use it only when a preference has been stated.

Mr and Esquire

There is often some confusion about the correct usage of 'Esquire'. Historically, the term denoted a person who attended a knight and, until recently, implied that the person addressed in this style was a landowner or had some professional status. In modern usage 'Esquire', generally abbreviated to 'Esq.', is used as a courtesy style, particularly in business correspondence. It should never be used together with 'Mr' or with a superior title, such as 'Professor' or 'The Hon'. When used, 'Esq.' is always placed after the name and before any honours, decorations or degrees. The writer chooses which form to use – whether 'Mr' or 'Esquire' – and should use it consistently in subsequent correspondence.

The forms of address for an untitled man are –

Written
ENVELOPE   Mr Nicholas Dolan
            or Mr N.V. Dolan
            or Nicholas Dolan, Esq.
LETTER
Formal   *Begin*   Dear Sir
            End   Yours faithfully
Social   *Begin*   Dear Mr Dolan
            End   Yours sincerely
Spoken   Mr Dolan

Master and Junior

'Master' is not generally used today in correspondence with boys. They are addressed simply by their full name –

Thomas Graves

Occasionally a need arises to differentiate between a father and son who bear the same name. This may be done by the addition of 'Junior' to the younger man's name –

> James Kirk, Jun., Esq.
> or Mr James Kirk, Jun.

Widows

After the death of her husband a woman is still addressed by her husband's name –

> Mrs Norman Moore
> Mrs N.T. Moore

The widow of the head of the family may be addressed as 'Mrs Moore', whereas other widows in the same family are styled 'Mrs Peter Moore', 'Mrs David Moore', and so on.

Divorced women

Following their divorce, women are addressed by their own forename although, if they so wish, they may retain their married surname –

> Mrs Fiona Worth

A divorced woman is entitled to keep her married name even if she or her former husband remarry.

Children of divorced parents

A child of divorced parents retains his or her father's name even if the mother remarries and changes her surname to that of her new husband. If, however, the father gives his permission, the new surname may be adopted. In certain circumstances a judge may give consent to a change of name.

Changing names

There are no strictly defined rules limiting a person's freedom to change his or her name. An individual's right to assume any name is valid in law if it is the name by which that person has become known by reputation or custom.

A change of name may be authenticated by one of the

following means –

1. *By private Act of Parliament.*

2. *By obtaining a Royal Licence. This is necessary if the change involves a change of heraldic arms.*

3. *By deed poll. This must be enrolled at the Central Office of the Supreme Court or in the College of Arms.*

A child under the age of 18 cannot change his or her surname without parental consent or without the permission of a judge. A forename may be changed at the time of religious confirmation, or another may be added when a child is adopted. The forename by which a person is known is not necessarily the first one that is registered. Kenneth Luke Newbury, for example, may be known to his family and friends as Luke, even though his signature may be K.L. Newbury.

Multiple surnames

If a family has more than one surname (some can have as many as four), it can be difficult to know the correct form of address for its members. It is more common for families with two surnames to use them both –

Ronald Boothby-Smith

Triple surnames, on the other hand, are often condensed to the last name only. Julian Barclay-Vane-Saville, for example, may be known simply as Julian Saville. This would be the everyday form of the family name, but formally, in announcements and on invitations, all three names might be shown. If in doubt it is better to include all the surnames than to shorten the name at all.

Extra surnames are often added where a family shares a surname with many others, such as Smith, Jones or Green. It has long been the tradition in Wales to identify families by additional surnames – Gareth Morgan-Davies, Geoffrey Price-Davies, and so on.

'Double-barrelled' names may evolve from the repeated use of a second forename within a family. After several generations have taken the name Ivor as a second name the

Brown family may adopt the name Ivor-Brown as their surname. Where a hyphen joins two surnames, it should be used in correspondence.

Joint forms of address

When writing to a husband and wife, the envelope bears both their names –

> Mr and Mrs Timothy Mayfield
> or Mr and Mrs T.J. Mayfield

A letter opens formally with –

> Dear Mr and Mrs Mayfield

and less formally with –

> Dear Tim and Mary

If one of the couple bears a title, the address should indicate this –

> The Reverend Anthony and Mrs Waters
> Mr Dennis Jamieson and the Countess of Shere
> Mr Barnaby and the Hon. Angela Simpson

Initials may be used instead of names where preferred –

> Colonel G.H. and Mrs Hemmings

If one partner has honours or decorations, this should be placed after the appropriate name –

> Sir Charles Atkin, K.C.B., and Mrs Atkin
> Mr Patrick Murphy and Dame Gladys Murphy, D.B.E.

. . . and family

When sending a letter, card or invitation to a couple and their children, many people address the envelope –

> Mr and Mrs F.D. Jarvis and family

This is not strictly necessary, as the wording inside could make it clear that all the Jarvis family are included in the greeting. If the children are over 18, invitations should be sent to them in their own right, even if they share the same address as their parents.

Unmarried partners.

In the past, people have hesitated to write the different names of a couple living together on an envelope. Social conventions were such that an element of pretence was advisable in certain circumstances. It was presumed that, if the postman knew a couple were unmarried, then it would not be long before this was common knowledge. Today such a need for tact seems out of place, but wherever there is a doubt it may be better to check that the couple have no objection to being addressed as individuals on an envelope –

Michael Blake and Nancy Kington

It could be the case that you do not know the surname of one of the partners. If all enquiries fail, it may be possible to get around the problem by addressing the envelope to the partner whose name you do know or by simply writing their forenames –

Michael and Nancy

The same applies to men or women who live together as a couple –

James Trenton and Mark Levine
Gail Grinley and Susan Lee

Single parents and their children

A child born outside marriage does not automatically take a surname, inherited from its parents. The child will only take his or her father's surname if the father is present at the time of registration, or acknowledges the paternity in a legally accepted form. The child may grow up using the mother's surname and assume it by reputation.

Professional names

It is common practice for people in the field of entertainment to adopt a 'stage name'. This is done for several reasons. It could be that another singer or actor has the same or a very similar name, and the change avoids confusion. Sometimes a person finds that his or her name does not reflect the correct 'image'. So 'Horace Bloggs' may become 'Storm Lionheart' on his way to rock'n'roll stardom, and an operatic soprano may change her name from 'Mary Smith' to 'Maria Sorrento'. These will be the names by which they will sign themselves in autograph books, but to family and friends they will remain 'Horace' and 'Mary'. In some instances, everyone gradually comes to use the stage name to avoid confusion.

In theatrical circles, married women rarely change their surname to that of their husband if their career and reputation have been based on their own or their stage name. If Georgina Brett marries Christopher Wing, for example, she will still be addressed in the theatre as 'Miss Brett', although privately using the style 'Mrs Wing'. This also applies to dancers, musicians and authors.

There are many women who prefer, for business or professional reasons, to retain their maiden name after marriage. This is their right, and there is no legal requirement for them to assume their husband's surname. After working for many years in a particular professional circle, the change to a married name might be problematical for some women, and the simplest answer is to keep their name for all practical purposes. It could also be the case that they prefer their own name and have no wish to change it.

Nicknames and abbreviated names

This can be a rather sensitive area. Nicknames are acquired for all sorts of reasons and are sometimes only acceptable when used by certain people. All of David Smith's friends and family may know, for example, that he calls his wife 'Hotlips'. However, as the nickname is quite personal to their relationship, it is accepted that he should be the only person to use it. Friends may also know that he calls his mother-in-law 'Dragonteeth', but nicknames not based on affection should never be repeated by others!

Traditionally, there are some surnames which are often

accompanied by a nickname: 'Chalky' White or 'Dusty' Miller are two examples. If someone indicates a preference to be called by his or her forename, then that preference should be honoured.

It should never be assumed that a person's name may be abbreviated, especially on a first meeting. If you know that someone is called Terence, that is how you should address him. Shortening a name is an indication of familiarity with a person, and it should not be presumed that it is acceptable to call him 'Terry'. If this is the name he prefers, the invitation should come from him.

Some people only shorten their names in certain environments. 'Maggie' may be known in her office as 'Margaret'. When speaking to her colleagues it is best to use the name by which they would normally address her.

Aunts and uncles

Although some people relish the idea of being called 'Aunt' or 'Uncle', there has been a growing tendency in recent years to drop these titles when a child grows up. Sometimes relatives may insist from the very beginning that a niece or nephew address them by their first name. If this is the case, the family should abide by their wishes.

If a younger person decides that he would prefer not to use the terms 'Aunt' and 'Uncle' then it is courteous for him to discuss this with the person concerned. 'Courtesy' aunts and uncles are occasionally created by parents who introduce old friends to a child as 'Aunty Gillian' or 'Uncle Kevin'. If Gillian and Kevin are charmed by their new titles, this is fine. If they look less than delighted, it is wiser to ask them how they would like to be addressed than to embarrass them every time they come to visit.

13. Letters, invitations and formal occasions

Personal correspondence

General points

There is little point in composing a well thought out and witty letter if it is written illegibly on flimsy scraps of paper. If you have taken the trouble to write to someone, your choice of stationery should reflect the nature of the correspondence. Although many people prefer the speed and immediacy of a phone call, there are times when writing a letter is unavoidable. It does have many advantages, however. You will have the time to choose exactly the right words to express your thoughts, and it can be as brief or as wordy as you wish it to be. You will not have to look for an excuse to ring off or be interrupted in your train of thought. The style of the letter will reflect your relationship with the person you are addressing. Close friends may not mind brightly coloured paper and an idiosyncratic style, but it is wise to retain certain formalities when writing to people who do not know you well.

Personal correspondence is usually handwritten, although many people do prefer to type if their handwriting is hard to read. If you choose to type a private letter, the greeting at the beginning and the signature should be in your own hand.

Plain white or lightly tinted paper looks stylish and is easy to read. The size is a matter of personal choice and depends to some extent on how much you wish to write. The envelope should match the paper both in size and colour. Black or blue ink should be used, and writing by fountain pen or fine-line pen looks better than ball-point. Pencil should never be used.

The address and date

The address is usually written in the top right-hand corner of the page –

34, Windmill Lane,
Harminster,
Sussex,
TF9 6BS.
Tel:

If the address is printed it may run along the top of the
page.

34, Windmill Lane, Harminster, Sussex, TF9 6BS
Tel:

The date is written beneath the address and is written in
full.

12th March 19—
or   March 20th 19—

Beginning a letter

The style you adopt for the opening of a letter depends on
how well you know the person to whom you are writing and
the nature of the correspondence. Letters to loved ones may
begin in any way that you feel appropriate – 'Dearest',
'Darling', etc. If you do not know the recipient, the style
should be formal, at least to begin with. If the reply is written
in a social style, the correspondence may then continue in the
same way. A formal beginning may be 'Sir', 'Madam', 'Dear
Sir' or 'Dear Madam'.

Sometimes a person may be known to you, but the content
of the letter may be formal. If, for example, you are writing to
your friend the mayor in his official capacity, the style of the
address should be 'Mr Mayor' or 'Dear Mr Mayor' rather
than 'Dear Fred'. This last form would only be used if the
letter is a personal one.

Friends and acquaintances may be addressed by their first
names only – 'Dear George'. There is a growing trend to
bridge the gap between this form of address and a more
formal style by including both the forename and surname –
'Dear Naomi Davis'. Should the recipient sign herself 'Naomi'
in her reply, it is acceptable to begin your next letter to her
with the forename only.

Ending a letter

The style of the beginning of a letter determines the appropriate way in which to end it. Very formal styles are not in use generally, but they are still found in particular instances. These include letters to royalty and to people in diplomatic services. Official letters to people in the armed services and in higher government circles may also require a very formalised style, such as –

I remain, (or I have the honour to be,)
My Lord,
Your Lordship's obedient servant

If 'Sir' or 'Dear Sir' has been used at the beginning, the letter should end 'Yours faithfully'. If the recipient is not known to the writer, but the content of the letter is not a business matter, it is acceptable to use 'Yours Truly'. If the letter is to a person known to the writer and it has begun with the use of the recipient's name, the correct ending is 'Yours sincerely'.

Personal letters may end in a manner which reflects your closeness to the recipient. This is entirely a matter of choice and is not governed by any rules of protocol. 'With much love' or 'With my very best wishes' are common endings to personal letters, and the variations are endless. Do make sure, however, that the style you adopt will not embarrass the person to whom you are writing. Generally speaking, simple direct language is preferable to any amount of flowery farewells.

Signatures

The signature should always be handwritten. If this is difficult to read, type your name underneath. A woman may like to add Miss, Ms or Mrs in brackets before the name to help the recipient in any further correspondence.

Style and content

It is relatively easy to write a social letter to a friend or relation thanking them for a gift or simply telling them your latest news. Many people find more difficulty with a letter which has a more negative or unhappy content, such as a refusal of help or a letter of complaint. It is beyond the scope of this book to go into detail about such letters, but here are some points which are worth remembering –

- *Do not use pompous or archaic terms where simpler ones would do.*
- *Sometimes bald statements of fact can sound unnecessarily hostile.*
- *Although later letters may be worded more strongly, the first letter regarding a problem should allow room for negotiation.*

The rules regarding the indentation of paragraphs are quite flexible. You may choose to begin each sentence against the left-hand margin of the page or to begin each paragraph further into the line; it is a matter of preference. Do, however, try to make use of paragraphs. This not only improves the presentation of a letter but allows the writer to organise his or her thoughts in a logical way. The final paragraph should contain a summary of the content of the letter and lead naturally into the ending phrase.

Writing invitations and replies

Written invitations are used for many social and formal occasions. The nature of the event usually dictates the style of the wording and the tone of the reply. Knowing the correct form of address in such circumstances helps to allay fears of 'doing the wrong thing', leaving you free to enjoy the event.

Royal invitations

An invitation from the queen or the queen mother is treated as a command. They are not sent directly from the sovereign but through officials, as follows –

- *An invitation to a state banquet is sent by the 'Lord Steward of the Household'.*

- *Functions which take place where the queen is resident and given by her are sent by the 'Master of the Household'.*

Replies should be addressed to the person who has sent the invitation on behalf of the queen and should be handwritten –

> General Sir Arthur and Lady Harvey present their compliments to the Master of the Household and have the honour to obey Her Majesty's Command to luncheon on November 9th at 12.30 o'clock.

- *Invitations to royal garden parties are sent by the 'Lord Chamberlain'. These do not usually require a letter of acceptance, but the admission card should be returned if the recipient is unable to attend. A royal command to attend a function is not refused without an exact reason being given –*

> General Sir Arthur and Lady Harvey present their compliments to the Master of the Household and much regret that they are unable to attend Her Majesty's Command to luncheon on November 9th owing to Lady Harvey's illness.

Other members of the royal family issue invitations rather than commands, but the reply should be sent to the member of their household who issued it.

Letters of thanks, where appropriate, are sent to the person who issued the invitation, with the request for the thanks to be conveyed to the member of the royal family.

Invitations to royalty

Correspondence and invitations to a member of the royal family are addressed to the 'Private Secretary'. Titles are shown in full –

> Their Royal Highnesses the Duke and Duchess of York

An invitation takes the form of a letter rather than a printed invitation. It is advisable to precede a formal invitation with a general enquiry in which the nature of the event would be outlined. The private secretary will advise those organising the function as to protocol and general arrangements for members of the royal family.

When a member of the royal family is to be present at a formal function, this should be shown on the invitation –

> In the gracious presence of Her Majesty the Queen
>
> In the presence of Her Royal Highness the Princess Royal

'Gracious' is used for the queen and the queen mother. Other members of the royal family are shown in their full style – 'His Royal Highness', and so on.

Invitations to official functions

The nature of the event should be made clear on the invitation, which is normally printed. The place, date and time should be included, with a finishing time where this is appropriate. Evening functions should always show the dress to be worn, and decorations, if required.

The Chairman and Governors of
The Institute of Cartographers
request the pleasure of the company of

. . . .

at their Annual Banquet
to be held at the Globe Hall, Scenic Street,
Birmingham
on Saturday 10th February, 1988,
at 7.30 for 8.00 p.m.

Evening Dress   R.S.V.P.
                                       The Hon. Secretary,
                                       17, Hill Street,
                                       Cliffden,
                                       Coventry.

Official invitations may include the office or name of the host, or both. Prefixes are not used except in the case of a privy counsellor who is not a peer. 'The Right Honourable —————' is used in this case.

Double invitations

Sometimes two people who are not husband and wife may be included in the same invitation. If they are mother and son, the form of address is 'Mrs Lionel Pritchley and Mr Ian Pritchley'. A brother and sister are styled 'Mr Anthony Hunter and Miss Carol Hunter'. Unmarried sisters are named as 'The Misses Forsyth'. If the invitation includes an un-named partner it may read –

> Mr Peter Kitchen and Lady
> or Miss Elizabeth Garton and Escort

Envelopes are addressed to the husband, if it is sent to his official address. Invitations sent to the home are addressed to the wife.

Replies to invitations to official functions

Acceptances may be worded as follows –

Mr and Mrs Harold Martin thank the Chairman and Governors of the Institute of Cartographers for their kind invitation for Saturday 10th February, which they accept with much pleasure.

The form of words may be varied. Phrases such as 'which they have the honour to accept' may also be used.

Declining an invitation may be done in the following manner –

Mr and Mrs Harold Martin thank the Chairman and Governors of the Institute of Cartographers for their kind invitation for Saturday 10th February, which they much regret being unable to accept owing to the illness of Mrs Martin.

The address should be included at the top of the paper and the date placed beneath the reply.

Invitations to private functions

Formal functions of a private nature, such as receptions and dinners, are usually printed or engraved on card.

'At Home' invitations bear the name of the hostess only. The names of the guests are written by hand in the top left hand corner.

```
┌─────────────────────────────────────────────┐
│ Nicholas ↝ Diane                            │
│                                              │
│                Mrs Edwina Scott              │
│                  at Home                     │
│                                              │
│             Thursday 24th March              │
│   R.S.V.P.                                   │
│   Hedgerows                      Cocktails   │
│   Staple Avenue,                             │
│   East Knapton                   7.00 p.m.   │
│                                              │
│                                              │
└─────────────────────────────────────────────┘
```

The host and hostess do not use a prefix before their names (such as 'The Worshipful'), or place any abbreviations after the name to show honours or degrees.

Sometimes an invitation may be extended on the telephone and followed up by a written invitation. There is no need to reply in this case, as this will have been done verbally. The card should bear the words 'To remind' and the R.S.V.P. be crossed out.

If a function is being held for a specific reason this should always be mentioned on the invitation.

If there is more than one hostess, their names are placed one under the other. The address for replies should be that of the hostess first named. Otherwise the addresses are placed across the page in the same order.

Replies to invitations to private functions

Replies are sent to the hostess only, even if they are sent from a husband and wife. If an unnamed guest has been invited, the reply should give the name of the person who is attending. If an invitation has to be declined, a reason should be given together with some expression of regret.

Wedding invitations

The most straightforward form of invitation is worded as follows –

Mr & Mrs Howard Eldridge

Mr and Mrs Edward Boothby
request the pleasure of
your company at the marriage
of their daughter
Sylvia
to
Mr Dominic John Harris
at St Stephen's Church, Mudeford
on Saturday 5th June, 1988
and afterwards at
The Three Crowns Inn

R.S.V.P.
Fairmeadows,
Green Lane,
Bournemouth

If the bridegroom has a title or rank this is included.

There may be necessary variations on this formula if the wedding is not hosted by the bride's father and mother. If the parents are divorced, the invitation would begin –

Mr Gerald Hyde
and
Mrs Grant Edwards
request the pleasure of
your company at the marriage
of their daughter
Glynis

. . .

If the wife has not remarried, the invitation would read 'Mrs Sheila Hyde'. If the bride's father or mother are the only host or hostess, the invitation reads 'his daughter' or 'her daughter', as appropriate.

Where the wedding is hosted by the bride's mother and stepfather the wording is –

Mr and Mrs Grant Edwards
request the pleasure of
your company at the marriage
of her daughter
Glynis

If the father and stepmother are hosting the wedding, the wording becomes –

Mr and Mrs Gerald Hyde
request the pleasure of
your company at the marriage
of his daughter
Glynis

Where other relations are hosting the wedding, the relationship between them and the bride is stated in the form of words used –

of their niece . . .
of her stepdaughter . . .
of his god-daughter . . . and so on.

If the bride is a widow, the invitation will read –

'Claire, widow of Mr Cecil Day'

A divorced woman will use the form 'Mrs Claire Day', unless she has reverted to her maiden name, when only her forename is used.

Occasionally a bride may host her own wedding –

Miss Roberta Jayston
requests the pleasure of your company
at her marriage to Mr James West

If an invitation is to the reception only, it reads –

Mr and Mrs David Gatsby
request the pleasure of your company
at the reception following the marriage
of their daughter Marion to Mr Gareth Smithson
at The Grange Hotel on Saturday 12th July 1988

Invitations to the ceremony only are worded in the usual way, with the omission of the details following the words 'and afterwards at'.

Replies to wedding invitations

Replies are written in the third person and should be sent as soon as possible after receipt of the invitation –

55, Napley road,
Upminster,
Essex

Mr and Mrs Richard Lawrence thank Mr and Mrs Bruce Warner for their kind invitation to the wedding of their daughter, Angela, on Saturday 16th October, and have great pleasure in accepting.

The reply should always be addressed to all the names in the invitation card and not just one of them. If there is a telephone number beneath the R.S.V.P., a written reply is not necessary as it may be confirmed by telephone.

Cancellations or postponements of weddings

There are occasions when it may be necessary to cancel or postpone a wedding. Announcements are usually printed on card. In the case of a postponement due to death or illness the reason is usually given –

Owing to the recent death of Mr Nigel Smythe, Mr and Mrs Godfrey Unwin deeply regret they are obliged to postpone/ cancel the invitations to the marriage of their daughter, Leonie, to Mr Anthony Smythe on 24th August.

If a new date has been fixed this may be included.

In the case of a broken engagement, the announcement might read –

Mr and Mrs Dennis Hopkirk announce that the marriage of their daughter, Margaret, to Mr Brian Porter, which was arranged for Saturday 18th May, 1988, will not now take place.

Formal occasions

Guests of honour

If the queen is a guest at a formal dinner, she is always placed at the centre of the table, with the host to her right. Other members of the royal family sit according to precedence (see Appendix 1). It is the custom at such an occasion to invite civic dignitaries, such as the lord lieutenant of the county, the lord mayor of the city or his equal or the high sheriff of the county. The seating plan for the top table should be submitted to the queen's private secretary for approval prior to the event.

On occasions where the queen is not present, the 'guest of honour' sits to the right of the host, and his partner to the left. The host's wife sits to the right of the principal guest.

Among the guests who should be seated at the top table are –
    Ministers of the Crown and privy counsellors
    Ambassadors and other diplomatic representatives
Important members of the inviting body may be seated at
intervals among the principal guests.

Other guests

Married couples at a formal dinner may be seated together or
apart. Wives are accorded the same precedence as their
husbands, unless they have superior precedence in their own
right. Precedence is normally only strictly observed at the
most formal functions.

The nature of the function may dictate the table plan to
some extent. If the numbers are quite small, the seating plan
may be displayed. Otherwise each guest should be given a
printed seating plan showing where he or she is to sit.
Wherever a list of guests is shown, there should be some
consistency in the use of prefixes and courtesy styles.
Decorations and honours should be shown, as well as any
academic abbreviations following the name.

Place cards, on the other hand, should be brief, and it is
not necessary to include formal prefixes. For example –

> Lord Marbury
> The Earl of Leicester

The exceptions to this are privy counsellors who are not peers,
who are styled 'The Right Hon.' The suffixes Q.C., J.P. and
R.N. should be included on a place card.

Speeches

The preamble to a speech should not be longer than the
speech itself! It is, however, important to remember all those
who should be specifically mentioned. Every function will
demand its own preamble depending on the guests present,
but the following are the most commonly used forms of
address.
The queen and the queen mother. In their presence the

preamble begins 'May it please Your Majesty'. Otherwise the host is the first person mentioned.

The president of the inviting body. If a royal guest is also the president of the inviting body, the form of address is 'Your Royal Highness and President'. Members of the peerage who hold the office of president are addressed as follows –

Duke or Duchess   Your Grace and President
Others   My Lord and President
If a Lady   Madam President

Chairmen who are members of the royal family are styled 'Your Royal Highness'. All other chairmen, including peers, are addressed as 'Mr Chairman' or 'Madam Chairman.'

Civic heads. Only the civic head of the city or town in which the function takes place is mentioned – 'My Lord Mayor', 'Mr Mayor', 'My Lord Provost', 'Mr Provost', 'Mr Recorder'.

The Archbishop of Canterbury – 'Your Grace'.

The Lord Chancellor – 'My Lord Chancellor'.

The Archbishop of York – 'Your Grace'.

The Lord Privy Seal – 'My Lord Privy Seal'.

The head of government – 'Prime Minister'.

Secretaries of state. A secretary is included only in the absence of the prime minister. He or she is addressed as 'Minister'.

High commissioners and ambassadors – 'Your Excellency(ies)'.

Dukes and duchesses – 'Your Grace(s)'.

Other peers, courtesy peers, and bishops – 'My Lord(s)'.

Other guests – 'Ladies and gentlemen'. If only one woman is present, the correct style is 'Lady and Gentlemen' or 'Mrs Harris, Gentlemen'.

Toasts

If toasts are to follow a meal, it is the custom that the first be made to 'The Queen'. At a very formal function or if a member of the royal family is present, a second 'loyal toast' may be made. This is addressed to 'Queen Elizabeth, the Queen Mother, the Prince Philip, the Duke of Edinburgh, the Prince of Wales and other members of the royal family.'

Smoking does not take place until after the loyal toast.

Appendices

1. Precedence

Precedence in England and Wales

Where an individual falls into more than one of the following categories, such as a bishop of London who is also a baron's eldest son, his position in order of precedence is that of his highest-placed category. The order may also vary according to the nature of the assembly in which he is participating, although the sovereign always has absolute precedence. The wives of office holders are also accorded the same precedence as their husbands, even if they do not share the title.

Men

(The sovereign)
(The Duke of Edinburgh)
The Heir Apparent
The sovereign's younger sons
The sovereign's grandsons
The sovereign's nephews
Archbishop of Canterbury
Lord High Chancellor
Archbishop of York
The prime minister
Lord President of the Council
Speaker of the House of Commons
Lord Privy Seal
High commissioners (of Commonwealth countries) and
   ambassadors of foreign countries
Dukes of 1. England
         2. Scotland
         3. Great Britain
         4. Ireland
         5. the United Kingdom and Ireland since the Union .

Ministers and envoys
Eldest sons of royal dukes
Marquesses (in the same order as dukes)
Eldest sons of dukes
Earls (in the same order as dukes)
Marquesses' eldest sons
Dukes' younger sons
Viscounts (in the same order as dukes)
Earls' eldest sons
Marquesses' younger sons
Bishop of London
Bishop of Durham
Bishop of Winchester
Other English bishops (according to seniority of creation)
Secretaries of state who are barons
Barons (in the same order as dukes)
Treasurer of the Sovereign's Household
Comptroller of the Sovereign's Household
Vice-Chamberlain of the Sovereign's Household
Secretaries of state who are not barons
Viscounts' eldest sons
Earls' younger sons
Barons' eldest sons
Knights of the Garter who do not have a title
Privy counsellors
Chancellor of the Exchequer
Chancellor of the Duchy of Lancaster
Lord Chief Justice of England
Master of the Rolls
President of the probate court
The Lord Justices of Appeal
Judges of the High Court
Vice-Chancellor of the County Palatine of Lancaster
Viscounts' younger sons
Barons' younger sons
Sons of life peers
Baronets according to the date of patent
Knights of the Thistle (without higher rank)

Knights Grand Cross and Knights Grand Commanders (in order)
Companions of Honour
Knights Commanders (in order)
Knights Bachelor
Official referees of the Supreme Court
Judges of county courts
Companions and Commanders (in order)
Members of the Royal Victorian Order (4th Class)
Officers of the Order of the British Empire
Companions of the Imperial Service Order
Eldest sons of the younger sons of peers
Baronets' eldest sons
Eldest sons of knights (in order)
Members of the Royal Victorian Order (5th Class)
Younger sons of the younger sons of peers
Baronets' younger sons
Younger sons of knights (in order)
Esquires and gentlemen

Women

The Queen
The Queen Mother
The Princess of Wales
The sovereign's daughter
Wives of the sovereign's younger sons
The sovereign's granddaughters
Wives of the sovereign's grandsons
The sovereign's sister
Wives of the sovereign's uncles
The sovereign's niece
Duchesses of 1. England
2. Scotland
3. Great Britain
4. Ireland
5. the United Kingdom and Ireland since the Union
Wives of the eldest sons of royal dukes

Marchionesses (in the same order as duchesses)
Wives of the eldest sons of dukes
Daughters of dukes
Countesses (in the same order as duchesses)
Wives of the younger sons of royal dukes
Wives of the eldest sons of marquesses
Daughters of marquesses
Wives of the younger sons of dukes
Viscountesses (in the same order as duchesses)
Wives of the eldest sons of earls
Daughters of earls
Wives of the younger sons of marquesses
Baronesses of England
Ladies of Parliament, Scotland
Baronesses of Great Britain
Baronesses of Ireland
Baronesses since the Union, life baronesses
Wives of the eldest sons of viscounts
Daughters of viscounts
Wives of the younger sons of earls
Wives of the eldest sons of barons
Wives of baronets
Wives of Knights of the Thistle
Dames Grand Cross of the Order of Bath
Dames Grand Cross of the Order of St Michael & St George
Dames Grand Cross of the Royal Victorian Order
Dames Grand Cross of the Order of the British Empire
Wives of Knights Grand Cross and Knights Grand
    Commanders in their correct order
Dame Commanders in their correct order
Wives of Knights Commanders in order
Wives of Knights Bachelor
Commanders in order
Wives of Companions in order
Wives of Commanders in order
Members of the Royal Victorian Order (4th class)
Officer of the Order of the British Empire
Wives of Members of the Royal Victorian Order (4th Class)

Wives of Officers of the British Empire
Companions of the Imperial Service Order
Wives of Companions of the Imperial Service Order
Wives of the eldest sons of the younger sons of peers
Daughters of the younger sons of peers
Wives of the eldest sons of baronets
Daughters of baronets
Wives of the eldest sons of Knights of the Garter
Wives of the eldest sons of knights
Daughters of knights
Members of the Royal Victorian Order (5th Class)
Members of the Order of the British Empire
Wives of Members of the Royal Victorian Order (5th Class)
Wives of Members of the Order of the British Empire
Wives of the younger sons of baronets
Wives of the younger sons of knights
Wives of gentlemen

Precedence in Scotland

After the royal family precedence in Scotland is as follows –

Lord-lieutenants of counties
Lord provosts of cities
Sheriffs Principal
Lord Chancellor of Great Britain
Moderator of the Assembly of the Church of Scotland
The prime minister
Secretary of state for Scotland (Keeper of the Great Seal), if a
    peer
Keeper of the Privy Seal, if a peer
Hereditary High Constable of Scotland
Hereditary Master of the Household
Dukes (as in England)
Eldest sons of royal dukes
Marquesses (as in England)
Dukes' eldest sons
Earls (as in England)

Younger sons of royal dukes
Marquesses' elder sons
Younger sons of dukes
Secretary of state for Scotland, if not a peer
Keeper of the Privy Seal, if not a peer
Lord Justice General
Lord Clerk Register
Lord Advocate
Lord Justice-Clerk
Viscounts (as in England)
Eldest sons of earls
Marquesses' younger sons
Barons and lords of Parliament (as in England)
Viscounts' eldest sons
Earls' younger sons
Barons' and lords' of Parliament eldest sons
Knights of the Garter
Knights of the Thistle
Privy counsellors
Lords of Session
Viscounts' younger sons
Barons' and lords' of Parliament younger sons
Knights Grand Cross and Knights Grand Commanders (in order)
Knights Commanders (in order)
Solicitor-general for Scotland
Lord Lyon King of Arms
Sherriffs Principal (when outside their county)
Knights Bachelor
Sherriffs Substitute
Companions of the Order of the Bath

From this point precedence follows that of England and Wales.

Local precedence

On civic occasions the rules of precedence are adjusted to incorporate civic heads. Within their own city or borough, lord mayors and mayors or their representatives (deputy mayors) take their precedence immediately after the lord lieutenant. Within the confines of the city or town hall, he or she is placed after members of the royal family. This applies also to a lord provost or provost in Scotland. Chairmen of district councils are treated in a similar fashion within their own district. Within the City of London the lord mayor of London takes precedence after the sovereign and before members of the royal family.

The basic rules of precedence may be adjusted wherever courtesy requires it. Guests of honour and important visitors may be placed out of precedence if this can be achieved without offense to others present. Wherever there is a doubt it is advisable to consult the representatives of the people concerned and obtain some consensus of opinion as to the correct form.

2. Abbreviations after names

Abbreviations placed after names should appear in a particular sequence, according to the following groupings.

1. Honours and decorations conferred by the queen

These are listed first. They have their own order of precedence, as follows –

Victoria Cross	V.C.
George Cross	G.C.
Knight of the Garter	K.G.
Knight of the Thistle	K.T
Privy Counsellor	P.C.
Knight/Dame Grand Cross, Order of the Bath	G.C.B.
Order of Merit	O.M.
Knight Grand Cross, Order of the Star of India	G.C.S.I.
Knight/Dame Grand Cross, Order of St Michael and St George	G.C.M.G.

Knight Grand Cross, Eminent Order of the Indian Empire	G.C.I.E.
Royal Order of Victoria and Albert	V.A,
Imperial Order of the Star of India	C.I.
Knight/Dame Grand Cross, Royal Victorian Order	G.C.V.O.
Knight/Dame Grand Cross, Order of the British Empire	G.B.E.
Companion of Honour	C.H.
Knight Commander of the Bath	K.C.B.
Dame Commander of the Bath	D.C.B.
Knight Commander of the Star of India	K.C.S.I.
Knight Commander of the Order of St Michael and St George	K.C.M.G.
Dame Commander of the Order of St Michael and St George	D.C.M.G.
Knight Commander of the Indian Empire	K.C.I.E.
Knight Commander of the Royal Victorian Order	K.C.V.O.
Dame Commander of the Royal Victorian Order	D.C.V.O.
Knight Commander of the Order of the British Empire	K.B.E
Dame Commander of the Order of the British Empire	D.B.E.
Companion of the Order of the Bath	C.B.
Companion of the Order of the Star of India	C.S.I.
Companion of the Order of St Michael and St George	C.M.G.
Companion of the Order of the Indian Empire	C.I.E.
Commander of the Royal Victorian Order	C.V.O.
Commander of the Order of the British Empire	C.B.E.
Distinguished Service Order	D.S.O.
Member of the Royal Victorian Order (4th Class)	M.V.O.
Officer of the Order of the British Empire	O.B.E.
Imperial Service Order	I.S.O.
Member of the Royal Victorian Order (5th Class)	M.V.O.

Member of the Order of the British Empire	M.B.E.
Royal Red Cross	R.R.C.
Distinguished Service Cross	D.S.C.
Military Cross	M.C.
Distinguished Flying Cross	D.F.C.
Air Force Cross	A.F.C.
Distinguished Conduct Medal	D.C.M.
Conspicuous Gallantry Medal	C.G.M.
George Medal	G.M.
Distinguished Service Medal	D.S.M.
Military Medal	M.M.
Distinguished Flying Medal	D.F.M.
Air Force Medal	A.F.M.
British Empire Medal	B.E.M.
Sea Gallantry Medal	S.G.M.
Queen's Police Medal	Q.P.M.
Queen's Fire Service Medal	Q.F.S.M.
Territorial Decoration	T.D.
Efficiency Decoration	E.D.

2. Royal appointments

Privy Counsellor (when it is used)	P.C.
Aide-de-camp	A.D.C.
Honorary physician to the Queen	Q.H.P.
Honorary Surgeon to the Queen	Q.H.S.
Honorary Dental Surgeon to the Queen	Q.H.D.S.
Honorary Nursing Sister to the Queen	Q.H.N.S.
Honorary Chaplain to the Queen	Q.H.C.

3. University degrees

The order in which degrees are shown after a name depends
on the custom of the awarding body. Generally speaking a
person holding a doctorate will not show any lower degrees. If
the holder of a doctorate is addressed as 'Dr ————', the
relevant abbreviation is not included after the name.

Doctor of Divinity	D.D.

Doctor of Laws	LL.D. (Cambridge and others)
Doctor of Civil Laws	D.C.L. (Oxford, Durham, Newcastle)
Doctor of Literature	D.Lit. (London, Belfast, Manchester)
Doctor of Letters	D.Litt. (Oxford and others)
Doctor of Letters	Litt.D. (Cambridge and others)
Doctor of Medicine	D.M. (Oxford)
Doctor of Medicine	M.D.
Doctor of Music	D.Mus. (Oxford and others)
Doctor of Music	Mus.D. (Cambridge and others)
Doctor of Philosophy	Ph.D. (Cambridge and others)
Doctor of Philosophy	D.Phil (Oxford and others)
Master of Arts	M.A.
Master of Laws	LL.M.
Master of Civil Laws	M.C.L.
Master in Dental Surgery	M.D.S.
Master in Engineering	M.Eng.
Master in Surgery	M.Ch.
Master in Orthopaedic Surgery	M.Ch.Orth.
Master of Commerce	M.Com.
Master of Surgery	M.S.
Master of Science	M.Sc.
Master of Music	Mus.M.
Master of Social Sciences	M.Soc.Sc.
Master of Theology	M.Th
Master of Veterinary Science	M.V.Sc.
Master of Gynaecology and Obstretrics	M.G.O.
Master of Fine Arts	M.F.A.
Master of Design	M.Des.
Master of Business Administration	M.B.A.
Master of Architecture	M.Arch.

Master of Metallurgy	M.Met.
Master of Education	M.Ed.
Bachelor of Arts	B.A.
Bachelor of Applied Science	B.A.Sc.
Bachelor of Business Admin.	B.B.A.
Bachelor of Business Studies	B.B.S.
Bachelor of Civil Engineering	B.C.E.
Bachelor of Surgery	B.Ch.
Bachelor of Civil Law	B.C.L.
Bachelor of Commerce	B.Com.
Bachelor of Divinity	B.D.
Bachelor of Dental Surgery	B.D.S.
Bachelor of Engineering	B.E.
Bachelor of Economics	B.Ec.
Bachelor of Education	B.Ed.
Bachelor of Law	B.L.
Bachelor of Letters	B.Litt.
Bachelor of Medicine	B.M.
Bachelor of Metallurgy	B.Met.
Bachelor of Pharmacy	B.Pharm.
Bachelor of Science	B.Sc.
Bachelor of Surgery	B.S.
Bachelor of Social Science	B.Soc.Sc.
Bachelor of Theology	B.Th.
Bachelor of Veterinary Medicine	B.V.Ms.

The abbreviations for honorary degrees are the same and are placed after the recipient's name. Degrees awarded by the Royal College of Art have the letters (RCA) following the abbreviation.

4. Religious Orders

African Missionary Society	S.M.A.
Assumptionists	A.A.
Augustinians	O.S.A.
Augustinian Recollects	O.A.R.
Benedictines	O.S.B.

Bethlehem Fathers	S.M.B.
Blessed Sacrament Fathers	S.J.S.
Calced Carmelites	O.Carm.
Camillians	O.S.Cam.
Canons Regular of the Immaculate Conception	C.R.I.C.
Canons Regular of the Lateran	C.R.L.
Cistercians	O.C.R.
Claretians	C.M.F.
Consolata Fathers	I.M.C.
Discalced Carmelites	O.D.C.
Divine Word Missionaries	S.V.D.
Fathers of St Edmund	S.S.E.
Franciscans (Friars Minor)	O.F.M.
Franciscans (Friars Minor Capuchin)	O.F.M.Cap.
Franciscans (Friars Minor Conventual)	O.F.M.Conv.
Franciscan Friars of Atonement	S.A.
Holy Ghost Fathers	C.S.Sp.
Institute of Charity	I.C.
Jesuits	S.J.
Josephites	C.J.
Marian Fathers	M.I.C.
Marists	S.M.
Mill Hill Missionaries	M.H.M.
Missionaries of La Salette	M.S.
Missionaries of the Sacred Heart	M.S.C.
Missionaries of Francis de Sales	M.S.F.S.
Montfort Missionaries	S.M.M.
Oblates of Mary Immaculate	O.M.I.
Pallottines Fathers	S.C.A.
Passionists	C.P.
Picpus Fathers	SS.CC.
Pious Society of St Charles	P.S.S.C.
Redemptorists	C.SS.R.
Sacred Heart Fathers	S.C.J.
Salesians	S.D.B.
Salvatorians	S.D.S.
Servants of the Holy Paraclete	S.P.

Servites	O.S.M.
Sons of Divine Providence	F.D.P.
Sons of Mary Immaculate	F.M.I.
Society of St Paul	S.S.P.
Verona Fathers	F.S.C.J.
Vincentians	C.M.
White Fathers	W.F.
Xaverian Fathers	S.X.

5. Medical qualifications and fellowships of learned societies

Medical qualifications are listed in the following order –
medical, surgical, specialities (such as obstetrics), qualifying
diplomas and other diplomas.

Honorary fellowships are usually the only ones included in
correspondence. Other fellowships (by subscriptions) would
only be included if writing to others in the same field.

6. Fellowships and memberships of professional institutions

The precedence within this group is usually dictated by the
importance of the fellowship or membership in the holder's
professional field.

7. Chartered societies

8. Appointments

These include Queen's Counsel (Q.C.), Justice of the Peace
(J.P.) and Deputy Lieutenant (D.L.).

9. The armed forces